"This book doesn't waste time on abstract theories—it shares specific suggestions on how we can create a sense of rapport, stay focused on solutions instead of fault, and motivate people to work together. Every classroom and library should have a copy."
—Tamara Hall, M.Ed., educational consultant and author of *When Life Kicks, Kick Back*

"As a former high school counselor, I can vouch for the need for this book. I've mediated so many conflicts that resulted from people not knowing how to talk to each other. I highly recommend that *Tongue Fu! at School* become a required text for teachers, students, and educational personnel. Everyone will benefit." —Joe Loverde, adjunct professor of education, Chapman University

"At the heart of how we relate to each other is how we communicate. The words of educators are especially potent, with the power to inspire children to reach for dreams or leave them mired in self-doubt. So what's an educator to do? Read Sam Horn's book! It provides critical guidance on how to communicate with respect and practice 'verbal diplomacy,' critical life skills. Must reading!" —Eileen Gale Kugler, author of *Debunking the Middle-Class Myth: Why Diverse Schools Are Good for All Kids*

"This book brings a smile to my face, because it is jam-packed with Sam Horn's welcoming warmth, wit, wisdom, and way with words. Every educator, parent, and student will resonate with these empowering principles you can put to use immediately." —Joel Goodman, Ed.D., director, The HUMOR Project, Inc., Saratoga Springs, New York

"As I work with schools across the nation on the issue of bullying, I realize that the reason students often behave so destructively is that they have not been taught constructive behavior. In *Tongue Fu! at School* , author Sam Horn provides that instruction. Schools interested in promoting peace and harmony among students, and creating a safe learning environment, would do well to adopt the techniques she delineates. I recommend this book to anyone who wants to promote constructive communication in their own lives and at all levels of our society." —Gaye Barker, coordinator NEA's Bullying and Sexual Harassment Prevention/Intervention Program

"A must read for educators, parents, coaches, club leaders, and anyone interested in helping kids become responsible, resourceful, resilient people who can act in their own best interest, stand up for values and against injustices, while respecting the rights and legitimate needs of others." —Barbara Coloroso, author of *Kids Are Worth It!*

"Want to empower the teens and teachers in your life? Buy them this book. It's packed with specific suggestions and fascinating examples showing how we can communicate to connect in the classroom, on the playground, and in the halls." —Eric Chester, founder of Generation Why, Inc. and coordinator of the *Teen Power* Book Series

"Don't put off buying this book! Plan on getting a copy for your child's teacher, principal, and school librarian; they'll thank you for it." —Rita Emmett, author of *The Procrastinating Child: A Handbook for Adults to Help Children Stop Putting Things Off*

TONGUE FU!™ at SCHOOL

30 Ways to
Get Along Better
with Teachers, Principals,
Students, and Parents

Sam Horn

A Scarecrow Education Book
TAYLOR TRADE PUBLISHING
Lanham • New York • Dallas • Boulder• Toronto • Oxford

This Taylor Trade Publishing paperback edition of *Tongue Fu! at School* is an original publication.
It is published by arrangement with the author.

Published by Taylor Trade Publishing
An imprint of The Rowman & Littlefield Publishing Group, Inc.
4501 Forbes Boulevard, Suite 200
Lanham, Maryland 20706

Distributed by National Book Network

Library of Congress Cataloging-in-Publication Data

Horn, Sam.
  Tongue fu! at school : 30 ways to get along better with teachers,
principals, students, and parents / Sam Horn.— 1st Taylor Trade Pub.
ed.
       p. cm.
  ISBN 1-58979-106-1 (pbk. : alk. paper)
  1. Interaction analysis in education. 2. Communication in education.
3. Conflict management. I. Title.
LB1034.H67 2004
371.102'2—dc22   2003025952

⊖™ The paper used in this publication meets the minimum requirements of
American National Standard for Information Sciences—Permanence of
Paper for Printed Library Materials, ANSI/NISO Z39.48–1992.
Manufactured in the United States of America.

"Teachers affect eternity. Who knows where their influence will end?"
—Henry Brooks Adams

May this book serve as a living legacy to my parents,
Warren and Ruth Reed, parents and teachers extraordinaire,
who served as the original source and role model for these principles.

This book is dedicated to them and to educators everywhere.

Thank you for all the work you do,
The hours you spend,
The caring you give,
The knowledge you share,
The wisdom you impart,
The curiosity you ignite,
The minds you open,
The cerebral sparks you fan,
The identities you nurture,
The confidence you build,
The hopes you inspire,
The dreams you encourage,
The creativity you foster,
The skills you teach,
The careers you launch,
The futures you shape,
The eternal influence you yield.

Contents

Foreword

T his book is not only long overdue, it is vitally important. We live in an age where discord, disrespect, and confrontation seem to be more and more the norm. Many of us are losing respect for one another and getting increasingly frustrated with unresolved conflict situations. Even worse, most people don't possess the skills necessary to help them resolve interpersonal conflicts when they arise. That circumstance not only negatively impacts life on a personal level, but it also negatively impacts the need for civility in American society.

The unadorned truth is that, now more than ever, we need each other. In the last decade, corporations have learned the hard way that sharing is more effective and productive than individualism, and cooperation and teamwork have surpassed cutthroat competition. That realization is no less true in other institutions of all stripes. It has finally dawned on these organizations that we cannot, and must not try, to go it alone or Lily Tomlin's description will surely apply: "We are all in this together by ourselves."

The new rules for organizations apply to individuals (it could be more appropriate stated the other way around). Tongue Fu! isn't about knowing what to say to someone in order to get even or come out on top. On the other hand, neither is it about turning and running—avoiding conflict at all costs. Tongue Fu! *is* about resolving conflict by knowing precisely what to say and do; it's about reaching out instead of putting down. It's learning to make the big stick an olive branch. Doing so will require seeking new partners and making new friends—sometimes with old antagonists. That isn't always easy, but remember this: You don't have to be in love to dance.

In many ways, it's a shame that these skills were never taught in school, but in this valuable book Sam Horn provides a specific road map for cooperation and conflict resolution. She gives practical examples of how to employ skills that most people never learned anywhere else—not in school, not from parents, not from employers. This book is not just for people of all ages, but a book whose message is ageless. Read, learn, and enjoy.

Don Cameron, executive director
National Education Association, 1983–2001
February 2004

"When you drink the water, remember the well."

—Chinese proverb

Acknowledgments

Anyone who has written a book understands why authors often thank a long list of benefactors. Friends, family, and colleagues sustain us during the months it takes to finish a manuscript. We are so full of gratitude when our project is finally finished that we want to make sure they know how much their wellspring of encouragement, good humor, and wisdom is appreciated.

So, heartfelt thanks to the following individuals. I feel privileged to know you, and I'm glad and grateful you're in my life.

Cheri Grimm, my sister and business partner, for her much-welcomed administrative talent, thoughtful people skills, balancing perspective, and for continuing to be there for me in more ways than I can possibly express.

Tom and Andrew Horn, my sons, for enriching my life, making me a proud mom, and for all your great stories about your school experiences.

School counselors Keith Adey and Scott Ertl for their brilliant suggestions on how we can make even more of a positive difference for students and fellow faculty.

Longtime friends, educators, and walking buddies Karen Danenberger, Fran Velasquez, Judy Gray, Christina Grimm, Mariah Burton Nelson, Rebecca Morgan, Sue Liebenow, and Ann Petrus for sharing your recommendations, editorial skills, and insights into human behavior.

John and Shannon Tullius, friends and founders of the Maui Writers Conference, for launching this world-class conference—and for jump-starting my enormously rewarding career as a published author.

Editor Tom Koerner and agent Laurie Liss for getting this project out of my head and into the hands of readers.

And to all the certified Tongue Fu! trainers for sharing this message of constructive communication with others. I join you in hoping that people use these techniques on a daily basis to forge win–win relationships with others.

Introduction

I n every Tongue Fu! program in the last ten years, someone will raise his or her hand and ask, "Why didn't we learn this stuff in school?"

Good question. We're taught the Three Rs (Reading, 'Riting, and 'Rithmetic), but we're not taught the important fourth and fifth Rs— Respect and Resolution. We're taught about verbs and adverbs; however, we're not taught that there are certain words that cause conflict. We study foreign languages; however, we don't study how to use our own language to get along better with others.

That's what this book is about. I believe learning how to treat each other with respect is just as important as math, science, and history. **Getting along with people is a byproduct of constructive communication, and it is a skill that can be taught. Not only can it be taught—it should be taught!**

Lee Iacocca said, "If you can't get along with people, you don't belong in this business, because that's all we have around here." Face it: If we can't get along with people, we may feel we don't belong anywhere. Are your interpersonal skills an asset or an albatross? Can you communicate in a way that commands the favorable interest, respect, and cooperation of the people you deal with?

As educators, we often tell students to "use your words." The problem is, many of us don't know what words to use to express ourselves and to resolve differences. As a result, we either get tongue-tied and say nothing at all, or we get tongue-twisted and say something that makes things worse. Neither reaction helps. That's where Tongue Fu! comes in.

Tongue Fu! Is Constructive Communication

"Once a human being has arrived on this earth, communication
is the largest single factor determining what kinds of relationships he makes with others and what happens to him."
—Virginia Satir

So what exactly is Tongue Fu!? First, let's clarify what it's *not*. I was
flying to New York as part of a Tongue Fu! media tour, and needed to
prep for a TV interview the next morning. I pulled my copy of the book
out of my purse to double-check a quote. A woman across the aisle from
me glanced at the cover, *grabbed* the book out of my hands and
exclaimed, "That looks interesting. Tell me what it's about!"

I answered with a smile, "Well, it's how to handle difficult individuals—
without becoming one ourselves."

"Ohhh," she said, "I wish I'd had that book on the plane before this
one. I was seated next to the most obnoxious man. I could have used
your book. I would have hit him with it!"

The Goal of Tongue Fu! Is to Create Cooperation

"What do you think of Western civilization?" —Reporter
"I think it's a good idea." —Mahatma Gandhi

Tongue Fu! is *not* about *hitting back*, getting back, getting mad, or
getting even. It is *not* about putting people in their place. It's about
putting ourselves in the other person's place so we can respond with
compassion rather than contempt. It is *not* about giving people a piece
of our mind. It's about giving ourselves peace of mind by being able to
handle challenging situations at that moment, instead of thinking of the
perfect response on the way home.

Tongue Fu! is a verbal form of Kung Fu!. Like martial artists, our
goal is to promote peace by deflecting, disarming, and defusing aggression. We don't go looking for fights, and if someone picks a fight with us,
we don't flail back and make things worse. We use our "martial arts for
the mind and mouth" to neutralize hostility and increase harmony.

Tongue Fu! is a civilized approach to communication. It is a form of
verbal diplomacy that helps us 1) focus on solutions rather than fault,

and 2) set a positive precedent for courtesy that motivates others to respond *in kind*. By using these integrity-based concepts, we can demonstrate to others that not only is it possible to work and live together cooperatively, it's advantageous for everyone involved.

Read It and Reap

"The object of education isn't knowledge—it's action."
—Thomas Kempis

I know you're busy, so this book doesn't waste time on abstract theories that don't work in the real world. Platitudes don't help much when someone is yelling at us or blaming us for something that's not our fault.

You're about to learn thirty ways to fast-forward through frustration, turn impatience into empathy, handle hassles with appropriate humor, think on your feet, keep your cool under fire, and continue to care—even if other people don't.

Each chapter is kept short so you can dip in and derive value, even if you only have a few minutes to spare. Program participants have asked that this book be written for both educators *and* students—so you'll find the examples and suggestions relevant whether you're a principal or professor, counselor or coach, teacher, tenth-grader, or parent of a tenth-grader.

Each chapter wraps up with an action plan and a Tongue Fu! tip for teens. It is my fondest hope that this book be used as a textbook in high school and college classrooms. People from all walks of life have told me they wished they'd learned this before. As one participant said regretfully, "If only I'd learned this sooner, I could have prevented so many hurt feelings, saved so many relationships."

A favorite teacher once told me, "A short pencil is better than a long memory." Please study this book with pen in hand. When you read an idea that's particularly relevant for you, write it on an index card and post it on your computer, class bulletin board, or refrigerator at home. You've heard the saying, "Out of sight, out of mind?" Keep these visual reminders "in sight, in mind" where you'll see them frequently throughout the day so you can hold yourself accountable for turning intentions into action.

Learn from Others

> "We should learn from the mistakes of others. We don't have time
> to make them all ourselves." —Groucho Marx

Thank you to everyone who so willingly provided the examples you'll find throughout this book. It's said, "A doctor is a shortcut to health; a coach is a shortcut to peak performance; a teacher is a shortcut to knowledge." These contributors generously agreed to share their mistakes and lessons learned in the hopes that their trial-and-error learning would be a shortcut to your success in getting along with others.

You may think Tongue Fu! is idealistic. It is, and it works. Thousands of Tongue Fu! graduates are proof that we can create less stressful, more satisfying relationships with others if we are willing to act with integrity and treat people with the respect they want, need, and deserve.

Ready to begin? Turn the page, and let's go.

PART I

Use Language that Establishes Rapport

"Sticks and stones can break my bones,
but words can break my heart."

—ROBERT FULGHUM

Language expert William Safire was once asked, "Is sloppy communication due to ignorance or apathy?"

His tongue-in-cheek answer? "I don't know, and I don't care."

Connect (vs. Cancel) What's Been Said

I think most of us do *care* about how we communicate. We *want* to get along with people. What we may not *know* is that we often use "trigger" words that cause people to feel criticized, cut off, blamed, or shamed. The next thing we know, we have an upset person on our hands, and that wasn't even our intent.

This section identifies several of the most commonly used trigger words and suggests how we can replace these "Words to Lose" with "Words to Use" so we can prevent conflict and promote cooperation.

Avoid Argumentative Words

"Words hang like wash on the line, blowing in the winds of the mind." —Rameshwar Das

While filling out some emergency contact forms at my sons' high school, I watched a situation unfold that showed the damage our first Word to Lose can cause.

A woman walked up to the counter next to me and told the administrative assistant, "My name is Rene Wilson. I have an appointment to see the principal."

The school secretary checked the principal's schedule and said, "Oh yes, Mrs. Wilson, I see you're scheduled to meet with him at 3:00, but he won't be able to make it."

Mrs. Wilson, perturbed, said, "But I set up this appointment a week ago. I took time off work to be here this afternoon."

The school employee said, "I'm sorry, but the principal was called away to an emergency school board meeting."

Mrs. Wilson persisted, "But why wasn't I called? I went out of my way to make time for this meeting. The least you could have done was notify me."

The school secretary replied, "I know, but the principal didn't even find out until a half hour ago . . ." and back and forth they went.

When I left, they were still arguing. Why? They both kept using the word *but*, which sets up a right–wrong interaction that turns discussions into disputes.

The Word *But* Antagonizes

"You can't build a relationship with a hammer." —Anonymous

Think about it. How would you feel if someone told you:

- "I hear what you're saying, *but. . . .*"
- "You did a good job raising your class's test scores, *but. . . .* "
- "I realize your students were looking forward to the field trip, *but. . . .* "
- "Yeah, we agreed to plant trees to have shade on the playground, *but. . . .* "

Do you see and hear how the word "but" cancels out what was said before? If someone uses a *but* when responding to us, they've just negated our point of view. If we use *but* when we reply to them, we've contradicted what they've said. That word is like a verbal hammer because it pits people as adversaries.

The Word *And* Acknowledges

"All the mistakes I have made, all the errors I have committed,
have been the result of action without thought." —office poster

What can we say instead so we don't end up arguing with people? We must think before we speak and replace the destructive word *but* with the constructive word *and*. The beauty of the word *and* is it acknowledges different points of view instead of arguing with them. Instead of setting up an either/or conflict, it lets each person's statement stand.

The school employee could have graciously expedited that situation by saying, "You're right, Mrs. Wilson, you did have an appointment with the principal, *and* I'm sorry he's not here to meet with you. He was called away for an emergency meeting. Would you like to reschedule for another time? And once again, please accept my apologies."

Look at the phrases below that now feature the word *and*. Imagine how different it would feel to be on the receiving end.

- "I hear what you're saying, *and* we tried starting PTA meetings at six and a lot of parents couldn't make it. Do you have any suggestions on how we could shorten the meetings so we're finished by eight?"
- "You did a good job raising your class's test scores, *and* we'll do an even better job improving their math skills."
- "I realize your students were looking forward to the field trip *and* then the prices of the bus went up. Do you have any ideas on how we could raise the extra money so we can afford to go?"
- "Yeah, we agreed to plant trees to have shade on the playground *and* then the company that was going to donate the trees backed out. Do you know any landscaping companies who might be willing to contribute a few saplings?"

The Word *And* Advances Conversations

"The happiness of your life depends upon the quality of your
thoughts." —Marcus Aurelius

The healthiness of our relationships depends on the quality of our language. You've heard the adage, "It's not what we say, it's how we say it"? Actually, it's both what we say *and* how we say it. While discussing this Word to Lose in a public seminar, a woman with a rather stunned look on her face spoke up. "I'm an English teacher. I've been telling students that *but* is a conjunction . . . for twenty-five years! I've realized it isn't a conjunction. It doesn't build on phrases; it blocks them out. 'I know this book is outdated, *but* it's on the reading list, so you're going to have to read it anyway.' 'Yes, it's Homecoming tonight, *but* you're still not getting excused early.' 'I realize you put a lot of time and effort into this essay, *but* it's full of typos.' Do you know what I just realized?" she said, still in a semistate of shock. "I've been teaching *English*. . . . I haven't been teaching *communication*."

Interesting distinction. We learn how to use past, present, and future tense, however we don't learn how to communicate with people so they don't take offense. Getting rid of *but* is one way we can stop needlessly offending people.

Turn Heated Debates into Discussions

"The test of a first-rate intelligence is the ability to hold two opposed ideas in the mind at the same time."
—F. Scott Fitzgerald

The test of a first-rate relationship is the ability of two people to hold opposing opinions at the same time *without* becoming enemies. It can be done as long as both people use the word *and* when stating their point of view. As soon as one person uses the word *but*, we're on our way to an argument because the implication is, "My way is better than your way, and your way is wrong."

From now on, if you and another person are quarrelling, take a minute to stop, step back, and think about what's happening. One or both of you is probably using *but*. Many of us are startled to discover we use *but* almost every time we speak. It's become a habitual space filler—something we insert between sentences without thinking. Once we became aware of how often we say it, we realize that by rebutting the other person's statement, we're not really listening—we're just waiting for our turn to talk so we can "prove" our opinion is better.

As soon as we substitute the word *and* for *but,* our conversations become less contentious and more courteous. Instead of trying to make people "see the error of their ways," we start treating their beliefs with respect. We may not agree with what they're saying; however, we see them as having a different point of view—instead of seeing them as being difficult.

A principal said changing this one word has made a great difference in his communications with faculty. "A teacher stormed into my office as soon as she received her class list, 'How could you do this to me?! I've got thirty kids in my class . . . and no teacher's aide!'

"I was about to tell her, 'Sorry, *but* our budget got slashed,' when I realized that wouldn't help. Instead I said, 'Yes, you were supposed to have an assistant teacher, *and* we won't be able to hire any additional staff. I'm sorry. I know you have a large class and deserve to have an aide.' She calmed down a little and said, 'But you promised I'd have help.' I told her, 'You're right, I did, *and* the district said no more hiring for the rest of the year. Please believe me, if there was anything I could do about this, I would.' Did the word *and* magically make the conflict disappear? No. Did it help it from becoming worse? Yes."

Language Matters

"Of course I'm yelling. That's because I'm wrong." —Leslie Charles

A school counselor told me, "I have a student who used to come in several times a week. He was either troubled *about* something or in trouble *for* something. He often had a hundred reasons why whatever was going wrong wasn't his fault.

"The first thing I did was point out a poster on my wall that has the word *BUT* in a big red circle with a slash through it, and let him know that word's not allowed in my office—and that goes for me too. In the beginning, he thought I was loo-loo; however after awhile he got into it because I let him catch me in the act.

"Instead of shooting down everything I said with '*But* he started it,' or '*But* the teacher's got it in for me,' the word *and* forced him to see things differently. He started listening instead of dismissing. If he was yelling, it forced him to think about what he was saying, which calmed him down. Instead of being defiant and taking exception to everything

I said, he started giving it a chance. Changing that one little word made such a big difference in his attitude."

Starting today, put yourself on high alert for the word *but*. When you find it on the tip of your tongue, Tongue Fu! it and use *and* instead. You'll find you can discuss emotionally charged topics without escalating into a fight. You'll both feel heard instead of hassled, and the two of you can move forward to a resolution instead of going back and forth trying to establish who's right and who's not.

Tongue Fu! Tip for Teens

I guarantee, if you keep using the word "but," you'll end up in arguments with teachers and parents because that word makes them feel you're making excuses. For example, "Yeah, I was supposed to bring my gym clothes today, *but*. . . . " Replace it with *and*, and they'll often back off and stop giving you a hard time because they'll feel you're being accountable. Try this instead, "I'm sorry, I know I was supposed to bring gym clothes today, *and* I'll make a note to myself to make sure to bring them tomorrow."

Action Plan for Connect (vs. Cancel)
What's Been Said

A student who was out sick the last week of the semester didn't turn in an important project and is going to fail the class. She feels she shouldn't be penalized because she was too ill to do her schoolwork. You feel it was her or her family's responsibility to at least contact the school to explain the circumstances.

Words to Lose	Words to Use
You use a trigger word that sets up a negative reaction.	You use a positive phrase to keep the conversation constructive.
"I heard a rumor that you had mono, but no one called me."	*"I'm sorry to hear you had mono, and if you need to miss school, it's your responsibility to contact us."*

Words to Lose	Words to Use
You use the word "but" which sets up an adversarial relationship because the other person feels you're not listening. *"I understand you were in bed, but you could have had one of your parents get in touch with us."*	You use the word "and" which acknowledges the other person's feelings and point of view and makes her feel heard. *"I understand you were in bed, and if something like this happens again, please have one of your parents call."*
You continue to use "but" which escalates this into an argument. *"I am listening, but the point is, even though you were sick, you still need a plan for getting the assignments done now."*	You continue to use "and" which moves the conversation forward to a resolution. *"I understand you were too sick to finish your assignments, and now I need to know your plan to complete your homework."*
You keep using "but" which makes the other person angrier. *"I do care, but I'm tired of hearing excuses."*	You keep using "and" which gives the other person incentive to cooperate. *"Okay, you'll have the essay done by Friday, and the book report by Monday."*

"We don't teach people by telling them what they did wrong. We teach people by telling them how to do it right."

—Tongue Fu!'ism

Coach (vs. Criticize) Performance

What do you do when students make a mistake? Do you tell them what they *should* have done?

This is a natural response, especially for educators and parents, because we think it's our job to point out mistakes so students can correct them. Please change this perception once and for all. Corrections come across as criticism. Telling students (or anyone) what they *should* have done makes them feel bad and doesn't teach or motivate them to do better.

Shape, Don't Shame Behavior

"When I'm right no one remembers; when I'm wrong, no one forgets." —Doug Harvey, baseball umpire

My teenaged son, Tom, walked in the house after his first on-the-road driving lesson and threw down his backpack. "How'd it go, Tom?" I asked. "What'd you learn?"

"I didn't learn anything," he said in frustration. "My driving instructor never says anything. He just sits there and waits for me to make a mistake, and then tells me what I did wrong."

"He doesn't teach you how to parallel park or anything?" I asked incredulously.

"No," Tom shrugged. "He never says a word unless I mess up, and then he jumps all over me and tells me I shouldn't have rolled through the stop sign or something like that. That's it."

What an unfortunate example of ineffective teaching. Not only was Tom not learning how to be a good driver, he was being turned into a Nervous Nelly who felt like he couldn't do anything right. Yikes.

Be a Coach, Not a Critic

"The secret of education lies in respecting the pupil."
—Ralph Waldo Emerson

Think about it. When people do something bad and we tell them what they *should* have done—they will resent us *even if what we're saying is true*. (A principal in New York once laughed out loud when I said this and added, "They will resent us *especially* if what we're saying is true!")

Why? The word *should* usually pertains to the past. Do you know anyone who can undo the past? People feel helpless when they are told what they *should* have done because they can't go back and erase their error. Even if what we're saying is true, it's tactless.

That's why, when people make a mistake, it's more constructive to focus on how they can handle this better *in the future*, ask how they're going to keep this from happening *from now on*, or suggest how they can do it right *next time*. By emphasizing or asking how they're going to do it correctly *next time* instead of scolding them for doing it incorrectly *this time*, we are *shaping* their behavior rather than *shaming* it. Now they are *learning* instead of *losing face*. This is the key to being a coach instead of a critic.

Look for the Lesson

"Nothing is a waste of time if you use the experience wisely."
—Auguste Rodin

When we tell students what they did wrong, they often retreat and withdraw. Our criticism crushes their spirit and curbs their curiosity. They don't want to risk looking like a fool, so they remove themselves from the "playing field" so they don't have to worry about being humiliated in front of peers. In school, that means they become reluctant to ask or answer questions because they don't want to chance looking "stupid."

A fundamental principle of teaching is "Reward the effort, coach the result." Instead of shutting students down by telling them what they were supposed to do or say, suggest a better alternative or use the Socratic method to guide them through an exploratory process so they can produce a better answer. That turns mistakes into insightful lessons instead of immobilizing failures, which is the essence of teaching.

We Don't Motivate People to Perform Better by Making Them Feel Bad

"Correction does much, but encouragement does more." —Goethe

A teacher told me, "It's not only students who don't like to be told what they *should* have done. That word triggers memories of my mom shaking her finger in my face and nagging me with, 'Lisa, you *should* have done this. You shouldn't have done that.' I have such a negative knee-jerk reaction to that word. I can't hear it without growling inside."

Do you have a similar reaction? Imagine someone said to you:

- "You should have turned in your attendance report after homeroom."
- "You should have brought that up in that faculty meeting."
- "You should have turned in your requests last Friday."

Chances are, you already know what you should have done, and these after-the-fact criticisms are the verbal equivalent of beating a dead horse. From now on, turn reprimands into recommendations. Imagine how you would feel if the above statements were rephrased as follows:

- "From now on, could you please make sure someone brings your attendance reports to the office right after homeroom?"
- "In the future, if you have questions about school activities, could you please bring them up in the faculty meeting? Other staff may

be wondering about the same things and we could clear up any confusion then."

- "Next time you need an overhead projector and screen, could you please submit your request to the office by the previous Friday so we can be sure to save one for you?"

See the difference? These more helpful responses suggest how to do it properly instead of rubbing our face in the fact that we did it improperly. They give us the incentive and information to try again, more efficiently. The word *should* chastises our poor performance, which leads to resentment, self-recriminations, regrets, retreat, and withdrawal. The words *next time, from now on*, and *in the future* allow us to save face (instead of lose face) and inspire us to improve our performance.

Mistakes Are Doorways to Discovery

"Man, did he make a wrong mistake." —Yogi Berra

A participant in one of my public seminars wasn't convinced. "What if a staff member's made an expensive error that's going to cost us a lot of time and money? If I don't point out the consequences of their actions, they won't understand the seriousness of the situation."

Once again, remind yourself that reiterating how badly someone blew it doesn't undo what happened and doesn't motivate them to take action—it motivates them to feel worse and to resent you for "dumping" on them. It may be tempting and temporarily satisfying to let off steam, however it could permanently damage your relationship because the target of your recrimination may never forgive you for making a bad situation worse.

An example of this idea in action happened when a new employee crashed the school's front office computer. The principal told me, "Not only did this woman lose all our files, she hadn't saved any of her work on a backup disc so we were going to have to re-create it from scratch.

"The *should's* were on the tip of my tongue, e.g., 'You *should* have told us you didn't know how to use the computer; and you *should* have left the system on instead of shutting it down.' Fortunately, in the heat of the moment I was able to remind myself that taking my frustration out on her wouldn't solve the problem. She knew what a mess she'd made, she didn't need me piling on and making her feel worse.

"Instead, I said, 'Tiffany, from now on, if you have any questions about the computer, please ask Barbara for help. She knows the system inside and out and can show you anything you need to know. Okay?'

"Tiffany apologized profusely and asked what she could do to make things right. She even volunteered to take computer-training classes so she could know how to use the system properly. Later that day, Tiffany came into my office and said, 'If I had done something like this at my previous job, my boss would *still* be yelling at me. That's why I left that school; I was always looking over my shoulder and living in fear of being chewed out for something. Thanks for treating me like a human being.'"

Don't Should, Suggest

> "It is a common mistake to think failure is the enemy of success. Failure is a teacher—a harsh one, but the best. Put failure to work for you." —T. J. Watson

What are you going to do next time someone around you does something wrong? Could you teach that person to put their mistake to work for them by focusing on what can be done about it *now*, instead of focusing on what should have been done earlier? Remind yourself and that individual that the only wrong mistakes are the ones we don't learn from.

A school counselor took exception to my point that *should* usually pertains to the past. She said, "I think we use the word to give advice. Like, 'You should take that SAT prep course if you want to apply to Tech.' 'You should be wearing a jacket. It's cold outside.' 'You should go to bed earlier. This is the second time this week you've fallen asleep in my class.' The problem is, kids tune this us out because it sounds like we're nagging.

"I consciously try not to use *should*. Kids who are in the rebellious stage will defy well-intended advice, even if it's to their advantage, because they're trying to be autonomous. Instead I say, 'If you want to apply to Tech, *it's in your best interests* to take that SAT prep course. It's guaranteed to raise your score one hundred points.' 'You *might* want to put on your jacket. It's cold outside.' 'You *might* want to get to bed earlier so you can stay awake in class.' Using words like *it's in your best interests*, and *you might want to* gives kids space to make up their own mind. They'll often choose to behave responsibly because this information is being presented to them as a suggestion and not as a command.

In fact, how to turn orders into requests so people choose to cooperate willingly is the subject of our next chapter.

Tongue Fu! Tip for Teens

One of the quickest ways to make friends mad is to tell them what they should or shouldn't have done. "You *should* have asked her to the dance earlier." "You *shouldn't* have been driving without your license." *Should's* come across as "told you so's." Chances are your friends already KNOW what they did wrong and they're not going to appreciate hearing it from you. Either hold your tongue (they won't miss your unsolicited advice) or ask, "What are you going to do about it now?"

Action Plan for Coach (vs. Criticize) Performance

Your child brings home a bad report card. You're shocked to see he has flunked math. You didn't have any idea he was having trouble with the subject. How do you talk to your son about this?

Words to Lose	Words to Use
You focus on the mistake and what he did wrong. *"Why didn't you tell me you were having problems?"*	You focus on the lesson and ask how he can make it right. *"What are you going to do to bring this grade up?"*
You use the word *should* and scold him for his error. *"You should have studied harder instead of watching TV."*	You use the words *from now on* and shape his behavior. *"From now on, the TV doesn't go on until homework's done."*
You continue *should'ing* on your son and criticizing. *"You should have asked your teacher for help if you didn't understand the assignments."*	You use the words *next time* so you're coaching. *"Next time you don't understand the assignment, what are you going to do differently?"*
You continue focusing on the past and he feels like a failure. *"I'm very disappointed in you."*	You focus on the future and he learns a lesson. *"What are you going to do now?"*

3

"A man convinced against his will is of the same opinion still."

—Anon

Turn Orders into Requests

D o you feel an internal growl when you're told you *have to* do something? Have you ever stopped to figure out why? Think about it. From the moment we wake up to the moment we go to bed, there are only two reasons why we do anything. We do things because we *have to* and because we *want to*.

If we do things because we *have* to (whether it's studying or filling out forms), we'll do them, but we'll probably be harboring the Three R feelings—Reluctance, Resistance, and Resentment. A workshop participant once piped up at this point and added, "If I'm given a command and I have to comply, I'll do it, but I'll do it with rage." Another attendee got in the spirit of things and chimed in with, "I'll do it with revenge." Glad we don't work with them!

Remember, the point of Tongue Fu! is to communicate with people in ways that set up rapport, not resentment. One way to do that is to rephrase orders into recommendations or requests to give people the incentive to comply because they *want* to.

Requests Give People the Incentive to Cooperate

"Common courtesy . . . isn't." —Tongue Fu'ism

20

Imagine being on the receiving end of these commands.

* "You'll have to wait. The vice principal's not in right now."
* "You need to turn in your travel receipts today if you want your expenses for that teachers' conference paid."
* "You need to clean up your classroom before you leave today. It's a mess."

Aren't those statements a little off-putting? Do you feel verbally "pushed around" by these types of abrupt instructions? Wouldn't you feel a little more receptive if they were reworded as below? These responses may take a couple more seconds to say, however couching them in courtesy gives the recipient motivation to cooperate willingly instead of complying reluctantly.

* "The vice principal will be back in about ten minutes. Would you like to wait or would you prefer to come back later?"
* "The deadline for turning in conference expenses is today. If you want to turn in your receipts, I'll make sure you get reimbursed for your expenses."
* "Could you please make sure your room is clean before you leave today?"

A skeptic once protested, "This is too soft. I'm not *asking* teachers to clean their room. It's not as if they have a choice. What if the health inspector is coming the next morning and our rooms really do need to be spotless?"

In this case, explain the urgency of the situation so the person understands it's the necessity of your request. By letting them know *what* needs to be done and *why*, instead of telling them what they need to do, they will feel like they're being treated with respect and they'll be more likely to snap to it. Say, "The health inspector will be checking every classroom first thing tomorrow morning and we want to pass with flying colors." Adding the rationale for your request will give them personal incentive to oblige.

Rephrasing Orders into Recommendations Gives People Autonomy

"There are few times in your life when it isn't too melodramatic
to say that your destiny hangs on the impression you make."
—Barbara Walters

It's not too melodramatic to say that the impression we make on others hangs on the words we use.

Autonomy is defined as "self-directing freedom," or "the quality or state of being self-governing." Everyone likes having the freedom to make his or her own decisions. Yet, teachers, counselors, and staff are often told what hours to work, what curriculum to cover, what meetings to attend, what people to work with, and on and on. These talented, hard-working adults, some with ten, twenty, thirty years on the job, have little say in how they function in their jobs. It can become enormously frustrating to be in a position where you are constantly treated as if you don't have a mind of your own.

That's why it is important to give people around us autonomy whenever possible. This is especially important when dealing with longtime employees and veteran staff. It's an insult to their intelligence and expertise to constantly be ordered around. And that's exactly what happens. There's a cumulative effect to arriving at school and being told what to do all day long. "You need to turn in your report cards by noon." "You have to keep the noise down in your classroom." "You need to monitor usage of the library computer. Students are accessing X-rated sites." "You need to schedule an IEP meeting with the speech therapist." It's enough to make you want to mutiny.

Dedicated professionals deserve to be treated with dignity. One way to do that is to ask for cooperation rather than giving autocratic commands. Turn, "You have to turn in your report cards by noon" to "Could everyone please turn in your report cards by noon today? We're going to enter the grades into the computer and send them out by Friday." Ask, "Could we all please step up our monitoring of Internet usage? We've received reports that some students are accessing X-rated sites, and we need to be a little more vigilant."

People Often Choose to Respond in Kind When Treated with Courtesy

"Life is not so short but that there is always time for courtesy."
—Emerson

An executive at an educational association said, "This was a real epiphany for me. As a manager, I always assumed it was my job to tell employees what to do. I never considered what it was like being on the receiving end of all those orders. You're right, by appealing to my staff's good judgment, they reward me by exercising it. I've also learned to use the word *we* instead of *you* when giving directives. Instead of saying, '*You* need to get your articles turned in for next month's magazine,' I'll say, '*We* need to get our articles turned in today for next month's magazine.' That's more inclusive and I don't come across as this controller who's arrogantly ordering them around."

He's right. When treated with respect, people often choose to do the right thing, not because it's being rammed down their throat, but because they see the wisdom of it. They will appreciate being treated like responsible adults—because it's so rare—and will often reward you by acting like responsible adults.

To Get Respect, Give Respect

"We awaken in others the same attitude of mind we hold toward them." —Elbert Hubbard

The Monday following a day-long program for a school district, I called a principal to follow up on a question that had arisen during our session. His assistant answered the phone and when I identified myself, she said, "You're Sam Horn?!" "Yes," I replied tentatively, not sure what was going on. She demanded, "*What did you do to my boss*?!" "I don't know, what?" I asked.

"I've worked for this guy for eight years," she said. "He's a barker. Every morning I come in, he has my 'to-do list' on my desk. Then, he barks at me throughout the day to make sure I'm getting it all done. 'Louise,'" she said, mimicking her boss's gruff voice, "'Get me that SOL report.' 'Louise, make sure that e-mail goes out to the school board.' 'Louise, I need the minutes from last week's faculty meeting.'

"This morning, my 'to-do list' was on my desk, as it has been every morning for the last eight years; however, he had added three little words to the top of it. Guess what they were?"

"Could you please?" I ventured.

"Yes!" she said gleefully. "Then, instead of barking at me all day long, he'd ask, 'Louise, could you please bring me that SOL report?' 'Could you please make sure that e-mail gets sent to the school board?' 'Could you please bring in the minutes from last week's staff meeting?' "

She said with heartfelt appreciation, "Working here is so much more pleasant than it used to be. Thank you."

Are you a supervisor who commands and demands? Are you a teacher who's fallen into the habit of ordering students around? Do the people around you see you as domineering? Could it be you're so used to telling people what to do, you haven't stopped to think of its demoralizing impact on others?

Try turning orders into recommendations and experience the receptivity created when commands are reworded into respectful requests. You'll discover people are much more likely to cooperate when they're treated with the respect they want, need, and deserve.

Yes, There Are Exceptions to These Rules

"Rules make good servants, but poor masters." —Anonymous

One parent protested with, "Aren't there exceptions to this? Aren't there times it's appropriate to give orders when something has to be done right away—no questions asked?"

Yes. There are times it's appropriate to give orders. A school bus driver once told me, "I'm not going to ask kids to take their seats. I'm going to tell them, 'Sit down!' I've got forty kids on my bus and I drive on city streets in rush hour. I don't have time to sweetly ask, 'Could you please stop hitting each other?' I'm going to yell, 'Keep your hands to yourself!' "

Good point. Please note that the ideas in this book are servants, not masters. I don't mean to speak in absolutes and say, *never* say this and *always* say this. Please make the ideas suit your situation.

Sometimes we need to be the voice of authority. Sometimes we need to "cut to the chase" and tell people precisely what they need to do. As James Thurber said, "Precision of communication is important . . . a false or misunderstood word may create as much disaster as a sudden thoughtless act." The point of this chapter, and of every chapter, is to communicate in ways that help us accomplish our goals. If your goal in a certain situation is to get immediate obedience, then an order may be, well, in order.

Chapter 20, "Lay Down the Laws," outlines some situations in which it's to everyone's advantage to establish and enforce rules. For now, the point is, are we needlessly alienating people by ordering them around, when we could instead let them know what needs to be done and why so they willingly choose to comply?

Tongue Fu! Tip for Teens

Does being told what to do make you grit your teeth and want to do just the opposite? The next time you "need" somebody to do something for you, take a couple extra seconds to phrase it as a request. If you tell your mom, "You have to buy me a new backpack. This one's broken," she might think, "I don't have to buy you anything!" If you tell your older brother, "You gotta help me with my calculus," he may think, "I don't have to help you with anything!"

Orders make people ornery. Their response is, "Who do you think you are, telling me what to do?!" Turn "have-to" demands into "would-you" requests, and people will be more likely to help you out. Ask your mom, "Mom, can we look for a new backpack this weekend? The straps are broken on my old one."

Ask your brother, "I know you're busy, but could you please take a few minutes to help me with my calculus?" Is a courteous approach guaranteed to get you what you want? No. It can get you *more* of what you want.

Action Plan for Turn Orders into Requests

You've been elected PTA president. This is the first meeting of officers and committee chairs and you want everyone to take responsibility for making this the most successful year ever. How do you handle your role?

Words to Lose	Words to Use
You assume being in charge means dictating orders and letting people know exactly what's expected. *"Listen up. Here's our agenda and you need to settle down and pay attention so we can finish on time."*	You understand that leading means treating people with respect so they're motivated to do their best. *"Thank you for coming. Let's stay on track tonight."*

Words to Lose	Words to Use
You tell people what they're supposed to do and they begin to resent your autocratic style. *"John, you're in charge of the Halloween carnival, and Sylvia, you're handling ticket sales."*	You phrase orders as requests and people appreciate you treating them with respect. *"John, could you please head up the Halloween carnival again? You did such a great job last year."*
You keep telling people what they have to do, and they feel bossed around. *"John, you need to call the community center and reserve it, and you need to make sure they give us a discount."*	You ask people for their help with the word "please" and they're motivated to cooperate. *"John, could you please reserve the community center and ask for a discount rate again?"*

4

"Kind words can be short and easy to speak, but their echoes are truly endless."

—Mother Theresa

Put Yourself on the Same Side

I magine you're the student council advisor and you're taking several students to a statewide leadership retreat for the weekend. You stop by the school office on Thursday and ask, "Can I pick up my paycheck early? We're leaving for the retreat first thing tomorrow morning," and the school bookkeeper brusquely replies, "No, you can't because it hasn't been processed by the district office yet."

Would you feel as if she's brushing you off? The words *can't because* are like verbal doors slamming in your face. Your request has been summarily rejected.

Now imagine that the bookkeeper had replied helpfully, "*Yes, you can* have your paycheck, *as soon as* it's processed by the district office. Why don't we give them a call, explain the circumstances, and see if they can speed things up?"

Wouldn't you have appreciated her "above and beyond" effort to grant your request? I once saw a poster that said, "There's not a lot of traffic on the extra mile."

From now on, when people make a request, instead of telling them why it can't be done, take a minute to figure out how it could be done. Go the extra mile and open the verbal door to a better relationship by replacing those rejecting words *can't because* with *sure, as soon as* or *yes, right after*.

Don't Alienate, Assist

"It is one of the most beautiful compensations of this life that no man can sincerely try to help another without helping himself."
—Ralph Waldo Emerson

The phrases *sure, as soon as* and *yes, right after* put us on the same side instead of pitting us side-against-side because they focus attention on how and when something *can* happen instead of why it *can't*.

A special education teacher named Rosario told me this simple concept turned around her classroom management. She said, "I have eight hyperactive children in my class. It seems all they ever want to do is have recess and art. They ask a hundred times a day, 'Can we have recess now? Can we get out our art supplies?' I used to explain, 'We can't go to recess because the bell hasn't rung' or 'You know we don't have art until last period.' Telling them 'no' would set one off on a tantrum, and the others would quickly follow.

"Your workshop helped me see that I was unknowingly (and unnecessarily) setting up an adversarial relationship. The next day when they asked, 'Can we have recess?' I'd say, 'Yes we can, as soon as the bell rings.' When they begged to have art, I'd say, 'Yes, we can have art when the clock gets to 1 P.M.,' or 'Yes, we can get out our art supplies as soon as you clean up your desks.'"

Think how often people at school ask for something and we tell them why it's not possible now—when it actually *is* possible later that day or as soon as another obligation is taken care of. Why set up a needlessly negative interaction by pointing out why their request can't be granted—and leaving it at that? Why not apply a little mental elbow grease and figure out how the request can be granted? This possibility thinking is a far better communication habit to develop and will pay off in more productive interactions.

Read the following examples to see how turning *can't because* into a *yes, as soon as* generates good will instead of ill will.

- **"Can we get this meeting started?"** Turn "No, we can't because not everyone's here yet" into "Yes, we can. We'll wait two more minutes for latecomers and then we'll get started."
- **"Can you tell us what's going to be on the test tomorrow?"** Change "Not now. You have to finish reading this chapter first" into "I'll be glad to, as soon as everyone finishes reading this chapter."
- **"I need to talk with the principal."** Change, "You can't go in there. She's in the middle of a parent conference" to "You're welcome to talk with her as soon as this parent conference is over."

Are You Standing in Their Way or Showing Them the Way?

"You can stroke people with words." —F. Scott Fitzgerald

I hope you're seeing a trend with these chapters. Words can be stumbling blocks or they can be stepping-stones. You can stroke people with words or you can strike people with words. It's in our own best interests to put some forethought into what and how we speak to others because it often determines how they respond to us.

Case in point: A program participant raised her hand while we were discussing this concept and said, "This is going to change the way I parent. I'm a single mother with three children under the age of ten. It seems all I ever do is tell them no. 'No, you can't play with your friends because you haven't done your chores.' 'No, you can't watch TV because you haven't finished your homework.' I feel so strict because it seems I'm constantly turning them down. What's worse is that when I tell them no, they start whining and I start 'stacking.' 'You know the rules around here. No TV until you've finished your homework! How many times do I have to tell you? When are you going to start listening to me?!' and off I go.

"You've made me realize that a lot of times, they *can* have what they want . . . as soon as. . . . Now, instead of telling them, 'You can't play with your friends because you haven't done your chores,' I'll tell them, 'Sure you can play with your friends, as soon as you finish your chores.

Pick up your room and take out the trash, and then you can go out and shoot hoops.' 'Yes, you can watch TV, right after you finish your homework. Do your math, let me have a look at it, and then you can turn on Simpsons (or Discovery Channel!).'"

She added, "This isn't just semantics. These responses change the whole dynamics of our relationship. When I tell them they can't do something, they see *me* as the big meanie blocking them from what they want. When I use these responses, *they're* the ones responsible for getting what they want."

Bravo. The whole point of Tongue Fu! is to make it easier for us to get along. Clearly, this switch in phrasing makes a major difference in whether we come across as agreeable or adversarial. Instead of being perceived as standing in a person's way, we're showing them the way.

Tongue Fu! Tip for Teens

Dostoyevsky said, "It seems as though the second half of a man's life is made up of nothing but the habits he accumulated during the first half." Have you ever stopped to realize that the way you're communicating now will become a lifelong habit? Ask yourself, "Is my communication helping me or hurting me?" Thankfully, it's not too late to start acquiring ways to talk to people that serve rather than sabotage your relationships.

Next time you're about to tell someone why you or they *can't*, stop for a minute and figure out how you or they *can*. For example, if a member of your study group asks, "Can you meet at the library at 3 P.M. tomorrow to research our project?" instead of just turning them down with, "I can't, I've got a baseball game," take it one step further and say, "My baseball game will probably go 'til 4—I could meet you at 4:30, though." Your friends (and parents and teachers) will appreciate your initiative in suggesting a workable solution instead of cutting them off with an answer that leaves them nowhere to go.

Action Plan for Put Yourself on the Same Side

You're the Student Activities Director and the class officers are talking about fundraising activities for the new school year. They're eager to begin their programs, however you need to be the "voice of reason" and remind them of the legal and financial responsibilities that must be met. How do you handle this sensitive role?

Words to Lose	Words to Use
You tell the students what they can't do, and they resent being shut down. *"I know you want to start selling candy on campus, but you can't until you get permission from the head office."*	You tell the students what they can do as soon as certain requirements are met. *"You can start that candy campaign as soon as you get permission from the head office."*
You list the reasons why they can't move forward with their plans. *"Before you buy the candy, you have to prepare a budget and prove that this will be a good investment that will pay off."*	You point out what they can do to move forward with their plans. *"You can contact the other high schools in the area to find out how much profit they produced."*
You continue to point out obstacles and they feel you're "raining on their parade." *"Plus, who's going to take care of all the litter when they throw the wrappers on the ground?"*	You continue to explain how they can achieve their goals and they feel encouraged. *"You might want to see if you can sell these through the concession stand at the game on Friday."*

5

"Words of comfort, skillfully administered, are the oldest therapy known to man."

—Louis Nizer

Turn Apathy into Empathy

Are you thinking, "What if there is no 'as soon as' or 'right after'?" What if *there's no way* I can give this person what they want? What if there's *nothing* I can do to grant their request?"

Good question. Guess what our next Words to Lose are? *There's nothing* and *there's no way*.

How would you feel if someone told you, "*There's no way* you're going to get a cost of living allowance"? Or "*There's no way* you can get into that class. It's full." "*There's no way* we can afford to set up a photo lab. It's too expensive."

Feels like a dead end, doesn't it?

From now on, if you have to deliver bad news, be sure not to use the words *there's nothing* and *there's no way*. Those words cause people to conclude you don't care . . . when the fact is, you probably do care—you're just not reflecting it in your language. What's worse, when people perceive you as indifferent to their situation, they often escalate their behavior in an effort to make you understand how important this is.

What can you say instead? This next story shows what a difference it can make when we respond to someone's plight with a helpful *there's something* instead of a helpless *there's nothing*. Instead of a hopeless

"*No way* I can change it," suggest a hopeful "Let's see if there's *any way* we can change it."

Let People Know You Care, Even If You Can't Grant Their Request

"People are lonely because they build walls instead of bridges."
—J. F. Newton

A teacher, Bev, had been looking forward to flying home for Christmas. Her parents were in poor health and she was afraid it was going to be their last chance to gather together as an extended family for their traditional family celebration. It was snowing when she left Washington, D.C., and by the time her plane landed in Chicago, a full-out blizzard was blanketing everything in white. Her connecting flight to Los Angeles had been grounded until the skies cleared. Stoic at first, she settled in with a good book and waited for the weather to get better. Three hours later, an airline employee announced the airport was closed for the rest of the evening.

Along with hundreds of other frustrated passengers, Bev lined up to find out what options she had. The beleaguered airline employee aggravated everyone's frustration with his rather abrupt, impersonal announcements. "All remaining flights have been cancelled. You'll need to rebook your flights for tomorrow."

When people protested that most flights for the next day were already full, he got testy and replied, "Look, don't blame me. There's nothing I can do about it. You're just going to have to be patient and make the best of it."

Yikes. There would have been a full-scale mutiny if he had continued with his "It's out of my hands" responses. Fortunately, a customer-service representative for the airline sensed the ugly mood of the crowd, took over the microphone, and made the following announcement. "First, please accept our apologies for this delay. We know many of you are trying to make it home for Christmas, and we wish we could make that happen for you. Unfortunately, the weather isn't cooperating. Please know we're going to do everything we can to book you on the first available flights. There's something we'd like to offer to make this situation a little more pleasant. We're issuing each of you a complimentary meal coupon so you can at least have a decent dinner on us."

With those words, the group's mood changed. Everyone was still stranded; however, they realized the airline employee was doing everything within his power to help them, and thus they stopped seeing him as the enemy.

Please note what happened in this situation, because it's important. There are times we have to disappoint others. There are times we have to deny legitimate proposals that deserve to be approved. If we shrug our shoulders and brush the person off with a perfunctory "There's nothing I can do," that person will probably get angry with us—they've got to get angry at something and we're the ones delivering the bad news.

If instead, we let them know what we wish we could do, what we hope will happen, we're building bridges instead of walls. People will be less likely to take their dissatisfaction out on us because they understand we're human. We cease to be the faceless, anonymous bearers of bad tidings and become caring human beings who are doing the best we can in the circumstances.

Give a Compassionate vs. a Dispassionate Response

"It is better to light one candle than curse the darkness."
—motto of the Christopher Society

I had an opportunity to speak at the 2003 National Association of Secondary School Principals convention in San Diego, California. While there, several principals told me one of the most frustrating aspects of their job is the district, state, and federal regulations that govern their every move. "That's the truth," another added with some exasperation. "When I first started out, we took field trips every other week, teachers created a lot of their own curriculum, and I had the freedom to hire and fire who I wanted.

"Now, I've got reams of forms to fill out, and it seems I'm constantly demotivating my staff by killing their initiative. A young teacher came to me all fired up with a really innovative idea for a classroom project, and I had to tell her we didn't have the money to fund it. I hated taking the wind out of her sails."

These principals agreed that the beauty of these "Words to Use" is that they convey the heartfelt empathy the principals feel for their faculty, even when they can't go along with what their teachers want. One principal said, "One of my counselors wanted to become certified in a bully-violence-prevention program. She even offered to pay for it out of her own pocket and use sick days so she could attend. I had to turn her down because of a policy that says her peers must have the same opportunity to attend the program. She probably thinks I didn't even 'hear' her because I just kept telling her there was nothing I could do.

"When I get back to school on Monday, I'm going to tell her, 'I hope you can take that training, because you deserve to go and I know it would help our school. There's something I'd like to suggest. Let's contact headquarters and explain you'll be sharing these skills with our staff when you return. Hopefully, we can convince them this is a worthwhile investment and they'll approve it.' Even if they don't," he told me, "At least she'll know I tried to support her initiative and good intentions.'"

Turn Verbal Dead Ends into Doorways

"If we were to make the conscious and frequent effort of treating others with consideration, the effects on us and on society as a whole would be amazing." —Henry Charles Link

One of my favorite Tongue Fu! success stories centers around this concept. A mother approached me at a break during our program to say, "I can't wait to get home to use this idea with my daughter." "Why?" I asked.

"I was in the kitchen last night preparing dinner," she explained. "My daughter came home from school, rushed into the kitchen, twirled me around, and said, 'I got it, I got it!'

" 'You got what?!' I asked, not knowing what she was talking about.

"She told me proudly, 'I got the lead in my high school play. Get out your day planner. I want you to circle this date and be there on opening night.'

"The date she indicated rang a bell with me. With a feeling of dread, I got out my planner, and it confirmed my suspicions. I shook my head regretfully, 'Honey, I can't be there. I've got a conference out of town that weekend. I'm leaving on Thursday and I'm not even getting back until Monday night.'

"She looked at me, hurt, and said, 'Mom, you travel all the time. You miss so many of my activities. Can't you make an exception this once?'

"I told her, 'Hon, this conference has been booked for months. There's no way I can back out now.'

"She persisted, 'This is really important to me. Can't you find someone else to take your place?'

"I said, 'There's no one who knows the program the way I do. I'm sorry, but there's no way I can be there at Opening Night.'

"My daughter left the room in tears. I realize now that she had no way of knowing how upset I was about having to miss her opening night. I just kept shutting her down by saying there was nothing I can do. She probably felt it wasn't a big deal for me, but it was. Tonight when she comes home, I'm going to apologize for the way I handled that. I'm going to let her know I wish I could be in the front row because I'm so proud of her. I'm going to tell her, "There is something we can do. Could we ask a friend to videotape your play so we can sit down on the couch together when I get home on Monday night and you can talk me through your performance?"

This story shows that though we can't always give people what they want, we can at least give them our concern. From now on, keep in mind that you can't always change the facts; however, you can change the way you deliver the facts, and that can change the way people respond to the facts. They may not like what we're telling them, but they'll be less likely to kill the messenger and more likely to accept our answer graciously if they know we care.

Tongue Fu! Tip for Teens

Have you ever had to turn a friend down, and she or he turned on you because you weren't "there" for them? One teen told me, "My best friend was running for student body president and wanted me to be her campaign manager. I had to turn her down because I was already over-committed with travel softball. When I told her there was no way I could do this for her, she accused me of not supporting her. I was hurt that she didn't understand where I was coming from. Now I see she felt I didn't understand where *she* was coming from.

"After talking with you, I called her up and said, 'I wish I had enough time to do a good job of being your campaign chair, and I don't because I'm either practicing or playing softball. There's someone I'd like to suggest. Jackie was junior class president, and she isn't running for office this time. She'd do a great job. Let's ask her.'"

You may be thinking, "This sounds like a lot of work. If this person were *really* my friend, she'd understand." Not. People can't read your mind. If you don't tell them with words how you feel, they won't know. Next time you have to tell a friend no, tell him or her you wish you could help out, and then suggest who might be able to. Your friend will appreciate your "thinking outside the box" and won't incorrectly conclude you could care less.

Action Plan for Turn Apathy into Empathy

You're the band director, and your award-winning band has been invited to participate in a nationally televised parade. It will cost a minimum of $150,000 to fly the group to the city, put them up in hotels, pay for meals, chaperones, ground transportation, and miscellaneous expenses. With less than three months notice, you conclude there is no way to raise that much money in that little time.

Words to Lose	Words to Use
You explain that there's no way the group can raise this amount of money that quickly. *"I know you want to go, but there's no way we can raise $150,000 in ten weeks."*	You tell the group you wish you could think of ways to raise this much money that quickly. *"I know you want to go, and I hope we can come up with some realistic ways to raise the cash."*
You appear apathetic because you keep pointing out the obstacles of why there's no way this can happen. *"Do you know how much money that is? There's no way each of you could come up with $1,500 to pay your own way."*	You come across as empathetic because you focus on the possibilities of how it could happen. *"I hope we can go, and I'm open to suggestions on how each of you can raise $1,500 so you can pay your own way."*
You deliver the bad news and let people know it's not your fault. *"Hey, don't blame me if we can't go. They should have given more notice."*	You ask people to brainstorm through the bad news. *"Let's figure out if there's any way we can make this happen."*

6

"We don't see things as they are, we see things as we are."

—Anais Nin

Preempt "Problems"

A program participant once asked, "Do you ever add words to your Words to Lose list?"

"All the time," I answered. "Got one in mind?"

"Yes," she nodded, "this word causes so many problems with my dean."

"What's the word?" I asked.

"That's the word," she said.

"What word?" I asked again, wondering if we were playing some kind of "Who's on first?" game.

"The word 'problem,'" she finally said. "Everything is a problem with him. If you go to his office and ask, 'Can I talk with you about something?' he'll say, 'Sure, what's the problem?' He wraps up every conversation and meeting with, 'Any other problems we need to address?' If you ask for permission to do something, he'll either say, 'Go ahead. I don't have a problem with that,' or 'No way, I've got a problem with that.' It's so bad that if you try to give him a compliment, he brushes it off with a 'No problem!'"

The Word "Problem" Gives the Perception Something's Wrong

> "All the mistakes I've made, all the errors I've committed, all the follies I've witnessed, have been the result of action without thought." —office poster

This woman brought up a good point. Many of us frequently (and habitually) use the word "problem," which gives people the impression something's wrong—even when it's not!

One of the purposes of Tongue Fu! is to speak *with* thought. Our goal is engage our brain *before* putting our mouth in motion. We want to take a moment to select and use words that will support what we're trying to achieve. It may take some time to change longtime habits; however, it will be worth the effort to do so.

The word "problem" usually undermines what we're trying to achieve because it makes the other person feel as if *they're* a problem. A school counselor was taken aback by this view. She told me, "I wish I could go back and re-do the last five years. When students are ordered to my office, I often start the conversation with, 'So, what's the problem?' It's done innocently, however I realize it gets us off on the 'wrong' foot. Starting the conversation with the word 'problem' reinforces the impression that *they're* a problem and the rest of the conversation unfolds accordingly. What's a better way to start things off?"

The answer to that is to use any words that don't give the "wrong" impression. Look at the juxtaposed responses following and see how the phrases on the left come across as accusing or assuming while the responses on the right ask for information or action in a more open-minded way.

A father shook his head regretfully while we were discussing this word in a workshop. "I wish I'd known about this sooner. My son's away at his first year of college. He called last night and after exchanging hello's asked, 'Dad, can I talk to you about something?' Guess what I said? 'Sure son, what's the problem?'

"I don't want to give the impression that the *only* reason he should call home is because there's a problem. By greeting him that way, that's the message I'm sending. From now on, I'm going to say, 'Sure, son,

"Austin, your teacher says you've been causing problems in class."	"Austin, talk to me about what's going on in Ms. Cole's class."
"I have a problem with your attitude. You need to stop being so disruptive."	"What are your ideas about how you can behave more cooperatively in that class?"
"You know what your problem is? You never think of anyone but yourself."	"Please be more considerate of the people around you."
"Any other problems we need to talk about before you go to your next class?"	"Anything else you want to talk about before you go to your next class?"
"You better not cause any more problems. I don't want to see you in here again."	"I'm counting on you to use good judgment. I know you can respond maturely."

what's going on?' to let him know he's welcome to call anytime, not just when something's wrong."

Change Your Words, Change Your Outlook

"Our life is what our thoughts make it." —Marcus Aurelius

A principal told me, "The day you spoke for our annual in-service program we had another speaker who talked about the importance of MBWA (Management By Walking Around). He told us if we are holed up in our office all day handling administrative work, we are not fulfilling our function as a manager because we are losing touch with our staff.

"That hit home with me because I often get buried under a stack of paperwork and answer dozens of e-mails every day. I vowed to get out from behind my desk at least once in the morning and once in the afternoon to roam the halls and connect with teachers and students.

"Guess how I greeted faculty members? 'Any problems?' No wonder it seemed like all I ever heard was complaints."

His story illustrates the point that our interactions are what our words make them. An Internet joke points out, "Just because you have a persecution complex doesn't mean people aren't out to get you." If we frequently use the word *problem*, it's easy to start seeing life and the people in it as "one problem after another." It's in our best interests to eliminate that pessimistic word and to use language that paints a more positive outlook.

Do You Not Have a Problem with the Word "Problem"?

"A powerful agent is the right word. Whenever we come upon one of those intensely right words, the resulting effect is physical as well as spiritual." —Mark Twain

A math teacher protested, "I don't understand why you're making such a big deal about this word. I use it all the time, and it doesn't cause any problems for me."

Interesting point. Scientists and mathematicians don't attach negative connotations to the word "problem." For them, the word simply means a puzzle that needs to be solved. In fact, they see problems as welcome intellectual challenges and they eagerly kick into overdrive in an attempt to figure them out.

If only we were the same. Scott Ertl, a gifted elementary school counselor in North Carolina, tries to help his young students adopt this more proactive approach to the word "problem." He told me about the time a young Chinese girl came into his office crying. He asked her, "What's happening?" (Notice he didn't say, "What's wrong?")

She said, "All the kids are teasing me because my eyes are slanted." The young girl, who had been adopted by an American couple, burst out with, "I hate being Chinese." Scott spent the next fifteen minutes talking her through a questioning process that helped her stop believing that being Chinese was a "problem" and start seeing it as something to be proud of.

Scott has produced a page of topics (e.g., weight, acne, body odor, being rich or poor, race, grades, glasses, being shy, teeth, name) that students might be sensitive about. They can check off the areas they're getting teased about, and then Scott talks them through a process that helps them get comfortable by knowing what to say so that area is no longer a "problem" for them. For more information about his gifted process of questioning, visit www.PlayShops.com.

Tongue Fu! Tip for Teens

A high school jock confessed, "If someone looks at me wrong, I come back with, '*What's your problem?!*' I understand now that those are fighting words. If they didn't have a problem with me before, they do now."

I asked him, "What could you say instead?" He thought about it for a minute, then grinned and offered this alternative. "How about, 'Whazzup?'"

Perfect! "Whazzup?" isn't an attack that puts the other person on the defensive (or offensive). It's a neutral question that engages instead of accuses.

Next time someone comes on a little strong, don't assume they're out to get you. Ask "Whazzup?" instead of "What's your problem?!" and you could be on your way to an understanding instead of an argument.

Action Plan for Preempt "Problems"

As the vice principal, you handle many of the disciplinary "problems" for the school. You've become aware, though, that the word perpetuates the perception that these young people can't do anything right. You're trying to change that. What do you do?

Words to Lose	Words to Use
You start off with the word *problem*, which establishes an adversarial atmosphere. "*I understand you've been causing problems in Ms. Cole's homeroom.*"	You start off by asking for help so the other person has the incentive to listen. "*Adam, why do you think Ms. Cole asked you to talk with me?*"

Words to Lose	Words to Use
You continue to use the word *problem*, which continues to focus on what's wrong. *"What's your problem anyway? You didn't used to get in trouble."*	You use words that don't give the "wrong" impression and focus on what can be done. *"This is out of character for you. What's happening?"*
You keep saying the word "problem" which perpetuates the frustration and doesn't fix what's not working. *"You'd better change your behavior or it will only cause more problems for you down the road."*	You deliberately avoid using the word "problem," which keeps your attention on solutions. *"It's important for you to show that you can be counted on to behave cooperatively."*

7

"Exaggeration is truth that has lost its temper."

—Kahil Gibran

Avoid Extremes

"You never listen to me!" "You're impossible to get along with." "Nothing ever pleases you." "Why does everything have to be your way?!"

Have you ever had these types of "all or nothing" claims tossed your way? How did they make you feel? Did you take exception to their excessive nature, which only caused the person to come back with more over-the-top accusations?

That's what extreme words do. They produce extreme reactions. Since our goal is to use language that helps rather than hurts, we want to avoid these inflammatory words. From now on, we are going to use words that accurately describe the situation instead of using sweeping generalizations that exaggerate and aggravate.

Turn Subjective Accusations into Specific Observations

"Precision of communication is important, more important than ever, in our era of hair-trigger balances, when a false or misunderstood word may create as much disaster as a sudden thoughtless act." –James Thurber

A recurring theme that has emerged from my interviews with educators is how much pressure they're under. An elementary school teacher told me, "It's only three weeks into the school year, and I'm already six weeks behind."

This dedicated teacher has thirty seven-year-old students in her class, and no assistant. She has several special needs children mainstreamed into her class and it is a full-time job just keeping order, much less trying to teach the Three Rs. Her day is a blur of interventions, trying to challenge and maintain the attention of students with vastly different comprehension levels, "herding" them in and out of the cafeteria within the allotted twenty-five minute lunch period, playing "therapist" to the emotionally needy, and supervising the playground during recess. Her day doesn't end at 2:15 P.M. She has IEP meetings, parent/teacher conferences, and staff meetings throughout the afternoon, and at least two hours of paper-grading and class preparation after dinner before she goes to bed.

Sound familiar? When we are stretched as far as we can go, it can be easy for extreme words such as "always," "never," "no one," and "every time" to come tumbling out of our mouth. Yet these inciting words would only serve to make an already overwrought situation more so.

What can we say instead? Specifically, describe what happened by using a number or date so you're dealing in facts, not inflated fiction. Or, ask yourself if the extreme word you're about to use is an inflammatory accusation (many are). If so, as we learned in chapter 2, suggest precisely what you do want instead of making a sweeping generalization about past behavior you don't want.

"Jose, I've told you a thousand times to stop slamming the door when you enter the classroom."	"Jose, please go back outside, and this time gently close the door behind you when you re-enter."
"I'm worried about how spoiled some of the students are. They never think about anyone but themselves."	"Let's talk about how we can set up some community service programs for the students."
"You *always* interrupt me. You *never* listen to what I have to say."	"Pam, please wait until I'm finished. I have more to say."

Use Objective vs. Subjective Language

"Tact is the art of putting your foot down without stepping on anyone's toes." —Laurence J. Peter

A teacher said, "I agree with what you're saying, and I try not to use extreme words. The question is, how can we tactfully keep other people from using extreme words with us?"

Next time, someone makes a sweeping accusation, simply ask, "*Is that true?*" and then be quiet. The beauty of that simple question is it holds people accountable. Asking people to substantiate what they're saying subtly forces them to admit they've overstated. This gets the conversation back to accurate assessments of what's happening instead of overblown reactions to what's happening.

There is another reason it's to our advantage to avoid using extreme words and to tactfully teach others not to use them either. Shakespeare observed, "There is nothing either good or bad, but thinking makes it so." In other words, circumstances themselves are not good or bad; we interpret them as good or bad. That's why it's in everyone's best interests to precisely describe what happened so our feelings match the situation. If we exaggerate our descriptions, we'll exaggerate our feelings, which exaggerates the consequences. If our portrayals are excessively negative, our outlook will be too.

Use Language That Fits the Facts

"Skepticism is not intellectual only; it is moral; a chronic atrophy and disease of the whole soul." —Thomas Carlyle

I've visually demonstrated this idea so you can clearly "see" how it works. First, let's clarify that *physical* events (i.e., we burn our finger or drop a stack of books on our toe) *directly* produce feelings. We don't have to think about, interpret, or decipher what happened—our finger or toe hurts.

Physical Event (We burn our finger.)		Feelings (We feel pain.)

Everything else that takes place (i.e., school is canceled for the day due to a heavy snow fall) is processed through our mind, which then produces feelings based on our values, expectations, history, and habitual attitude and language. You may feel glee if you're a student, ("Yippee, a snow day!"), frustration if you're a teacher, ("Oh no, we're going to get further behind"), or dismay if you're the district supervisor making this decision. ("This is a can't win situation. If I cancel school, I'm going to get called a wimp, and if I don't cancel, I'm going to be accused of endangering the children.") At this point, the feeling isn't a reflection of the event itself, it's a reflection of your interpretation of that event.

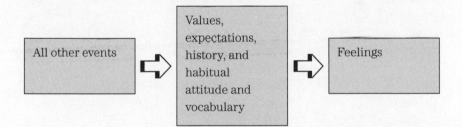

What's this mean? It means people who habitually use extreme negative language start seeing "everything" as a disaster because their interpretation of events is customarily pessimistic. Cynics and skeptics who use gloomy "all or nothing" words see the world as a bleak place because events are colored through their dark lens.

This was the case with a cafeteria supervisor who had a habit of "catastrophising." She told me, "I got this from my mom when I was growing up. She was always leaping to worse case scenarios and working herself into a tizzy over nothing. If it was cold and rainy outside, she'd tell me I better bundle up or else I'd get a cold that could turn into pneumonia. If I was late coming home, she'd immediately conclude I had run my car off the road and was lying somewhere in a ditch, all alone and mortally wounded.

"It wasn't until I saw your 'Am I Reacting or Responding?' grid that I understood how often I do the same thing. Just yesterday I was telling my husband, 'It's *impossible* to please those kids. I work myself to *death* trying to create nutritional meals and *all* I *ever* hear are complaints. *No one ever* appreciates how hard I work to serve decent food on the paltry budget I'm given.'"

She continued, "I see how often I talk myself into a funk. Is there a way to turn this around?"

Overreacting? Ask Yourself, "Is This True? What Is True?"

> "I've suffered a great many catastrophes in my life. Most of them never happened." —Mark Twain

I told her, "From now on, when something happens, keep your 'first thoughts' honest by asking yourself, 'Is this true?' Imagine you go out of your way to prepare a new dish and a few unappreciative kids in line take one look at it and turn up their nose with, 'Eyuh! What's that?! Meat surprise?' Perhaps your first thought is, 'I knew it was a waste of time experimenting with that new menu. I should just stop caring.' Ask yourself, '*Is* it a waste of time experimenting with new items? Should I stop caring? Is any of that true?' Well no, it's not true. Then, ask yourself, 'What is true?'

"Well, what's true is that three kids out of three hundred dissed your new dish. What's also true is that several came back for seconds. What's true is that it gives you pleasure to try new menu items and that most of the kids liked the new casserole. Do you see how asking yourself 'Is that true?' and 'What is true?' helps you use phrasing that more accurately fits the facts—which produces feelings that more accurately reflect the facts?"

Am I Reacting or Responding?

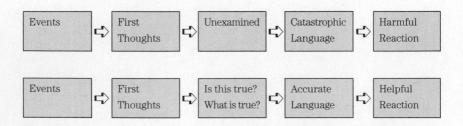

I told her, "Place this 'Am I Reacting or Responding?' grid where you can see it throughout the day. Next time something happens and you're about to react, stop for a minute. Run what you're thinking and about to say through the grid above. Ask yourself, 'Will that reaction help or hurt?" If it won't help and it could hurt, why not replace those extreme words with what's true so you keep the focus on the facts?

Take Responsibility for Your Responses

"The willingness to accept responsibility for one's own life is the source from which self-respect springs." —Joan Didion

Although the words "react" and "respond" are sometimes used interchangeably, I make a distinction between them in this book. The word "react" is the root of the word "reactive" which is defined as "occurring as a result of stress or emotional upset." The word "respond" is the root of "responsible" which is defined as "able to answer for one's conduct; able to choose for oneself between right and wrong; marked by or involving accountability."

One of the goals of Tongue Fu! is to *respond* to events and other people's behavior instead of *react* to them. Our first thought to people yelling, complaining, or accusing is rarely positive. If we go with our first thought, which is usually based on the stress or emotion of the moment, our incendiary reaction will add fuel to the fire and we'll be on our way to a verbal brawl.

If, instead, we take a moment to run our first thought through the "Am I Reacting or Responding?" grid, we can often transcend our initial "base instincts" and produce a more rational response. In doing so, we hold ourselves and others accountable for responding appropriately to events instead of letting emotions run away with us. A bonus is that by conducting ourselves responsibly, others will be more likely to follow suit.

Tongue Fu! Tip for Teens

Has anyone ever told you the words you use have a direct and profound effect on how you see the world and how others see you? Do you say things like, "I'm going to *kill* my little brother when I see him."

"I look *terrible* in this dress." "I'm going to *wring his neck* for keeping this from me." "I'll just *die* if he doesn't ask me to the prom."

Those are such over-the-top words. Number one, they make us sound like drama queens. Number two, we're conjuring up violent images while describing causal, everyday occurrences.

One teen said, "Come on, why are you making such a big deal about this? Everyone talks like that. It doesn't mean anything."

That's precisely my point. It *does* mean something. Words matter. What we say counts. Are you really going to die if Andrew doesn't ask you to the prom? Then why say it? Why not run that phrase through the "Am I Reacting or Responding" grid? Doing so will help you realize that while you'll definitely be disappointed if he doesn't ask you, life will go on. Do you see how running extreme language through this grid puts thinks (intentional play on words) in perspective? Next time you're getting upset or feeling depressed, ask yourself, "Is what I'm thinking/saying true? What *is* true?" Those two questions can keep you from "catastrophising" and making "thinks" worse than they really are.

Action Plan for Avoid Extremes

A curriculum specialist has a reputation for "awfulizing." You have been assigned to an accreditation team with her and you're not looking forward to being around her "doom and gloom" attitude. How do you handle her frequent complaints?

Words to Lose	Words to Use
She starts in with a sweeping generalization about how awful everything is and you *react*. *She says, "Nothing ever goes right for me. This is the last thing I need right now."* *You say, "Don't start. I don't want to be here either."*	She starts in with a sweeping generalization about how awful everything is and you *respond*. *She says, "Nothing ever goes right for me."* *You say gently, "Nothing . . . ever goes right for you?" with your eyebrows raised.*

Words to Lose	Words to Use
She continues to use extreme words and you continue to add fuel to the fire.	She continues to use extreme words and you choose not to add fuel to her fire.
"These accreditation trips always happen at the worst possible time. I was already behind and this is going to make it worse."	*"These accreditation trips always come at the worst possible time."*
"I know. I'm going to have to work 24/7 to make up for this."	*"It's true that they put me behind for a couple weeks, but I think it's worth it."*
She keeps catastrophizing and you get fed up and let her have it.	She keeps catastrophizing and you hold her accountable.
"I hate getting assigned to these. I'd rather be anywhere than here."	*"I hate getting assigned to these. I'd rather be anywhere than here."*
"Your complaining is getting on my nerves. Put a sock in it."	*"Is that true? You'd rather be anywhere than here?"*

8

"The surest way to make someone worry is to tell him not to."

—Joe Moore

Take the "Nots" out of Your Communication

One of the most important points in my book *ConZentrate: Get Focused and Pay Attention When Life Is Filled with Pressures, Distractions, and Multiple Priorities* (St. Martin's Press, 2000) is that it's hard for our mind to focus on the opposite of an idea. The mind is literal. It imprints and acts on what it is told, not on what was *intended*.

Are you wondering, "What's this got to do with Tongue Fu!?"? Many of us frequently use the words "not," "don't," "stop," and "won't" when giving instructions or orders. We may tell a fellow teacher, "You better *not* be late again." We might warn a classmate to, "Stop teasing me." We might try to reassure a student before her public speaking presentation, "There's no need to be nervous."

Unfortunately, the mind overlooks the words "not," "don't," "stop," and "won't," and locks onto whichever word in the sentence is most prominent and visual.

Want an example? Say, "I'm going to the grocery store." Your mind probably flashed an image of your local market. You may have even pictured yourself pushing a shopping cart through the aisles, selecting items off the shelves. Now say, "I'm *not* going to the grocery store." Chances are you still mentally pictured your local A & P, Safeway, or Piggly Wiggly because the words "grocery store" were dominant in that sentence.

You see what's coming, right? Since the words "not" "don't," "stop," and "won't" are usually coupled with negative orders, we end up imprinting, reinforcing, and perpetuating negative behaviors. Look at the phrases below. Which words jump out? Which do your mind focus on?

- "Stop yelling. You're making too much noise."
- "Don't run through the halls. You could hurt yourself."
- "You're not lying to me, are you?"
- "I don't want to see you picking any more fights."
- "I'm not going to cry. I'm not going to cry."
- "Don't make me put you in detention."
- "Stop laughing at her. That wasn't funny."
- "Don't report this to your union rep. It'll just make things more complicated."
- "I don't want to give you the wrong impression."

Focus on the Desired Behavior vs. the Dreaded Behavior

"The New York subway system is odd. They have these big 'No Spitting' signs everywhere. I never even thought of spitting until they brought it up, then it was all I felt like doing."
—comedienne Paula Poundstone

Yikes. Do you see how the phrases above keep attention on the very thing we don't want? Have you ever been skiing down a slope and told yourself, "I hope I don't fall." Falling may not have been on your mind before, but once you mentioned it, it was all you could think of!

That's what happens when we give ourselves or others negatively phrased orders. From now on, be sure to use language that centers attention (yours and other peoples') on the *preferred* course of action.

How do you do that? Simply ask yourself, "What do I want?" and then state that. We'll talk more about *picturing* desired performance in chapter 27, "Act Confident Even When You Don't Feel Confident." For now, you can increase the likelihood of producing hoped-for behavior (vs. harmful behavior) by rephrasing the previously listed statements like this:

- "Please lower your voices and quiet down. We need silence for this test."
- "Please walk through the halls. We want you to stay safe."
- "I want the truth. Tell me exactly what happened."
- "Give each other space and keep your hands to yourself."
- "I'm going to keep my cool. I'm going to hold my head up high."
- "I will tell you this once and only once, so listen up."
- "Apologize to Celia, and speak to her with respect from now on."
- "Let's see if we can work this out ourselves."
- "I want to make a good impression because I'd really like to get this job."

Turn Don'ts into Do's

"Don't find fault, find a remedy." —Henry Ford

We can modify Ford's insight to say, "We find what we look for. If we look for faults, we'll find faults. If we look for remedies, we'll find remedies."

This same concept applies to the words "don't," "won't," "stop," and "not."

As long as we keep coupling them in our communication with what we don't want, we'll keep getting what we don't want. If we start communicating what we *do* want, we'll get more of that.

A football coach told me, "This is so obvious. What's embarrassing is how often I get it wrong. Last Friday, we played our crosstown rival for homecoming. We were down at the half and I gathered the team around me for a little pep talk. I wish I could take back what I said. I told 'em, 'Don't quit on me now. You don't want to disappoint all these fans who showed up tonight. We have to play no-mistake football. No fumbles or interceptions, okay? We're not beat yet.' Argghh! I don't have to tell you what happened. We lost the ball three times due to fumbles and interceptions and got beaten."

Hopefully, next time the coach will pepper his pep talk with words and images that fill his team's mind with their *ideal* performance so *that* becomes what they picture and perform. "Keep giving 100 percent. I'm confident you can turn this around. We're going to control the ball, make first downs, and score points. Let's go out there and win this game. I know you can do it."

You Get What You Expect

"Life consists of what a man is thinking, all day long."
—Ralph Waldo Emerson

A woman e-mailed me after a seminar to contribute her own lesson-learned about this idea. She wrote, "I'm the single mother of a daughter who's in her first year of college. This is the first time she's been away from home by herself, and she's all the way across the country. I was a nervous wreck. She has several night classes and I was worried sick something bad was going to happen to her walking back to her dorm on that dark campus. Every time we talked, I'd tell her a hundred times to be careful.

"The last time she called, I was reminding her to be cautious (again!), when she interrupted and said, 'Mom, you think worrying about me is a way of showing you love me. To me, worrying just shows you don't trust me.'

"I was stunned into silence. I realized she wasn't saying this to hurt me; she was saying it to let me know she was a big girl and could take care of herself. I promised I wouldn't worry anymore, but of course, the more I told myself not to worry, the more I worried!

"Then, I remembered what we talked about in your seminar. Instead of focusing on what I *didn't* want to do, I was supposed to focus on what I *wanted* to do. It took me awhile to come up with a substitute, but finally I realized what I was supposed to do was trust her, just like she asked me to. So I decided to fill my mind with the belief that she was safe and thriving in her new environment.

"In the beginning, I kept slipping back into my old habits. 'I hope Katie's not walking on that campus late at night by herself.' Oops. 'I'm going to trust that Katie's doing just fine. She's a smart girl. She knows how to keep herself safe.' Slowly but surely, I'm changing from a worry-wart into someone who has faith in my daughter's good judgment."

As educators, you're probably familiar with the research showing that students perform up—or down—according to their teachers' expectations.

Students also perform up or down according to their teachers' language. From now on, get the "not's" out of your communication and make a concerted effort to use words that plants behavioral seeds of what you *would like* rather than what you *wouldn't like*. Everyone involved will benefit as a result.

Act on Your Intentions to Use "Words to Use"

"Knowing is not enough, we must apply. Willing is not enough, we must do." —Goethe

After discussing all eight Words to Lose, a program participant spoke up, "I can't remember all this. Am I supposed to write all these on my hand and stop people mid-sentence so I can refer to my 'crib' notes on my palm?"

I smiled at his timing and asked him, and the rest of the group, to refer to the back page of their workbook. There was a page of reminder sheets for them to duplicate, laminate, and post on their bulletin board, computer, or desk. As pointed out in the introduction to this book, keeping these ideas "in sight, in mind" can help us follow up on our good intentions to apply these ideas to our daily interactions.

In fact, one of my favorite success stories comes from a good friend and fellow author, Mary LoVerde, (*I Used to Have a Handle on Life, but It Broke*). Mary, a fabulous speaker and mom, called one evening and said, "Sam, I have to tell you what happened. Emily came home from a school dance an hour *after* curfew. You know Emily. Normally she's very responsible, so I was in a panic. I tried to call her cell and it was switched off. When she finally came home, I was so relieved I lost it. 'Emily, where have you been?!'

"Emily tried to explain, 'I'm sorry, Mom, I just lost track of time. By the time I figured out how late it was, I thought I better get home as fast as I could.'

Mary said, "I was so wound up, I just kept venting. 'I thought something terrible had happened,' and on and on I went.

"Emily got frustrated because she had already apologized, so she started telling me to get off her case. In the middle of all this, my eyes fell on the list of Words to Use we keep on our refrigerator. I stopped, collected myself, and said, 'Emily, from now on, please keep your cell phone with you. And if for some reason you're going to be more than five minutes late, please call us and let us know what's happening so we know you're okay.'

"Emily said simply, 'Okay, Mom.' And that was the end of it. A few minutes later, she went to bed and called from the stairs, ''Night, Mom.' I called back, ''Night, Emily.' If I hadn't seen that reminder card, I probably would have still been unloading on my daughter. She would have gone to bed mad, I would have gone to bed mad, we would have woken up mad, the tension could have lasted for days. I had to call and tell you, these Words to Use work!"

Ready to put these Words to Use to work for you? Visit www. SamHorn.com for information on how to get Words to Use Reminder Cards for yourself and your staff. Post them where you'll see them throughout the day. *Before* you send that e-mail, check your language against the language list of do's and don'ts. Could you reword it so it's kinder? Could you rephrase those orders into questions so the other person has more incentive to cooperate?

Refer to your list before you walk into a meeting to discuss a challenging situation. Could you eliminate the *shoulds* and *buts* so you set up connection rather than conflict? Are you making sure not to use extreme words so the other person doesn't take offense? Could you use friendly phrases so the other person is more likely to *respond in kind*? The extra time it will take for you to plan and phrase your communication diplomatically will be well worth it.

Tongue Fu! Tip for Teens

A high school student told me, "My best friend is dating this jerk. We used to be close, but now that she's spending all her time with him, we don't have much in common. I've tried warning her he's a loser, but she just shuts me down. What you said makes me realize I'm just pushing her further away by harping on how she shouldn't be wasting her time with this guy. I think she needs me to believe in her more then she needs me to tell her she's throwing her life away. It doesn't help to tell her she's going to end up flipping burgers at some fast-food joint while the rest of us are at college. I'm going to call her tonight and let her know I'm still there for her."

Do you have a friend who's getting into trouble? Are you telling her what she should NOT be doing? Instead of jumping on the bandwagon and telling her what she's doing wrong, be the one friend who continues to believe in her. Your support could be a verbal life raft that helps her live up to your expectations instead of living below everyone else's.

Action Plan for Get the "Nots" out of Your Communication

You're a bus driver who somehow has to keep your eyes on the road and drive through rush-hour traffic while, at the same time, keeping sixty-six rambunctious kids under control. How do you handle this?

Words to Lose	Words to Use
You tell the kids what you don't want them to do, which means that's exactly what they do. *"Hey, you two in back. Stop hitting each other."*	You tell the kids what you want them to do which sets a positive precedent. *"Nick, switch seats with Rosa and keep your hands to yourself."*
You yell at the kids to stop misbehaving, which perpetuates their misbehavior. *"If you don't stop causing trouble, I'm going to throw you off the bus."*	You firmly tell the kids exactly how you want them to behave. *"Kids, sit down and be quiet the rest of the way."*
You focus on what they should not do, so they continue to cause trouble. *"You're nothing but trouble. You better not hit her again."*	You say what you'd like them to do, so they act in accordance with your trust. *"Boys, I know you can act like young gentlemen."*

PART II

Create a Climate of Cooperation

"If we were to make the conscious and frequent effort of treating others with consideration, the effects on us and on society as a whole would be amazing."

—HENRY CHARLES LINK

9

"Treat people as if they were what they ought to be,
and you help them become what they're capable of becoming."

—Goethe

Fast-Forward through Frustration

What's your first reaction when someone is rude to you? Are you tempted to be rude back? While that reaction may be understandable, it will only make matters worse. Why? Returning their rudeness reinforces an antagonistic atmosphere and escalates negative emotions.

Our goal, as stated earlier, is to think *before* we speak and to use language that soothes ruffled feathers instead of ruffling them up more. This chapter offers several techniques that can help you turn exasperation into empathy so you can respond with compassion instead of react with contempt.

Ask Yourself, "How Would I Feel?"

"If you want others to be happy, practice compassion. If you want to be happy, practice compassion." —Dalai Lama

61

Please think of someone who frustrates you. (A woman in a seminar piped up with, "Just one?!") Would you like to know how to get past your impatience with this person? The next time someone's getting on your last nerve, ask yourself, "*How would I feel* . . . if this was happening to me?" "*How would I feel* . . . if I was in their shoes?"

Most of the times we're frustrated, we're only seeing things from our point of view. We're thinking, "Why are you taking this out on me? I'm not responsible." We're thinking, "No one treats me this way and gets away with it." We're thinking, "This is the hundredth time I've been asked that question today." As long as we continue to consider only how we feel, we will remain frustrated.

The beauty of these questions is they cause us to see the other person's point of view. We may not *like* or *agree* with their behavior; however, putting ourselves in their place helps us understand it. That understanding gives us the incentive to be sympathetic instead of sarcastic.

Want an example? A school secretary, who had attended a Tongue Fu! program the week before, was "woman-ing" the office by herself while her coworkers were at lunch. As luck would have it, the phones started ringing off the hook. Sheila had to put several callers on hold.

When she finally got to the last caller, she started to apologize for the delay. However, she didn't have time to get the words out because the caller started in, "How dare you put me on hold! I'm calling long distance from a pay phone, and you made me wait ten minutes." The caller kept venting, and Sheila started feeling more and more put upon. She thought to herself, "Hey, I'm doing the best I can. You have no right to yell at me!"

Then, she remembered to ask herself, "*How would I feel* if I had called the school long distance from a pay phone, and was put on hold for ten minutes? I wouldn't be very happy about it either." That insight gave her the patience to continue to be courteous. Instead of giving in to her initial urge to return the caller's rudeness, she fast-forwarded through her frustration and used the AAA Train (which you'll learn about in chapter 10) to resolve the woman's complaint.

Turn Exasperation into Empathy

"The more a man knows, the more he forgives." —Confucius

A man had occasion to use the "Empathy Question" ("How would I feel?") with his mother, and it changed their relationship for the better. He explained:

"My mother has been in a rest home for the last couple years. It had gotten to the point where I dreaded driving out to see her every Saturday because all she ever did was complain. She complained about her roommate. She complained that no one ever came to see her. She complained about her aches and pains. I had to force myself to visit because she was so unpleasant to be around.

"When you brought the Empathy Question up in our workshop, I asked myself, 'How would I feel if I were in bed eighteen hours a day, seven days a week? How would I feel if I lived six feet away from someone I didn't even like, and that person played the TV so loud I couldn't even hear myself think? How would I feel if days went by and none of my children had an hour to come and visit? How would I feel if every morning I woke up, my joints hurt because of my arthritis, and I couldn't see a day when that wasn't going to be the case?'

"Asking 'How would I feel?' moved me out of my frustration. When I took the time to consider what my mom's days were like, and when I stopped to think of all she's done for me, I realized it's the least I can do to spend a couple hours listening to her."

Empathy Helps Us Be Proactive Rather than Reactive

"Many a friendship is lost for lack of speaking." —Aristotle

A variation to Aristotle's quote is, "Many a relationship is lost for lack of empathy." Relationships are doomed if both parties stay focused solely on their own needs, wishes, and feelings. Think about the situation above. This man was becoming more and more disengaged and his mother was becoming more and more isolated. He saw her as being unpleasant and she probably saw him as being unsympathetic. Can you see that as long as they only saw their own side of the issue, their estrangement would only grow worse?

The power of asking "How would I feel?" is that the resulting insight gets us out of the self-absorbed justification of our feelings. Instead of experiencing only our annoyance with the other person, we experience the root cause behind their behavior. The resulting epiphany can either help us be more tolerant of their behavior, or motivate us to do things differently so they no longer act or behave that way. Either way, our empathy transforms the situation.

Ask Yourself, "Why Is She or He Behaving This Way?"

"If you are patient in one moment of anger, you will escape a
hundred days of sorrow." —Chinese proverb

Patience is indeed a virtue. However, if we are empathetic in one moment of anger, we will escape even more days of sorrow.

There's a follow up to the story of the man becoming more empathetic to his mom's situation. He said, "You had told us in our program that Tongue Fu! was proactive, not reactive. You said we could continue being frustrated about what we didn't like, or we could create or request what we would like. You had said, 'If you don't like your mother complaining, what *would* you like?' I realized that what I wanted was to talk about our happy memories. Asking myself, 'Why does she complain so much?' made me realize *she didn't have anything else to talk about.* You suggested I take a photo album with me next time I visited her because Queen Elizabeth had said, 'Good memories are our second chance at happiness.'

"That next Saturday, I took our family photo album. One picture of this crazy uncle of ours had us laughing so hard, tears were streaming down our faces. A picture of a mountain cabin we used to visit every summer brought back a whole hour's worth of memories. Figuring out *why* my mom complained all the time, instead of getting fed up with her complaining all the time, turned that situation around."

It's to Our Advantage to Transcend Antipathy

"Make yourself a blessing to someone. Your kind smile or pat
on the back just might pull someone back from the edge."
—Carmelia Elliott

Please think of someone or something at school that bothers you. A teacher took my ConZentrate workshop because she had several children with ADHD (Attention Deficit Hyperactivity Disorder) in her class. Sandy said, "I didn't feel like a teacher, I felt like a warden. It was almost impossible to accomplish anything because I spent most of my time trying to keep them from destroying the classroom—or each other. I was constantly telling them to sit still and keep their hands to themselves. I was exhausted by the first recess and they were still raring to go."

Fortunately, Sandy's school showed a video called Fat City (produced by Public Broadcasting and available by calling 800-344-3337) during a weekly staff meeting. The documentary is filmed from the perspective of someone whose hyperactive brain is constantly on the go. The camera flits from one thing to the next, mimicking what it's like to have a mind that's always on the move.

"Before I saw that film," Sandy confessed, "those kids were really getting to me. Seeing that film was such an eye-opening experience. I told one of the boys that watching that twenty-minute film with its crazy camera angles, blurry focus, and constant switching from one object to the next made me dizzy. He looked at me with an 'I told you so' look and said, 'Now, you know what it's like for me. That's how I feel *all the time*!'

"After experiencing what it's like for them, I have more compassion. I've adjusted my teaching style to keep them engaged. I realized that if they were physically distant they'd be mentally distant, so I've seated them up front so I can keep their attention. I'm not saying everything's perfect, it's better than it used to be."

Ask Yourself, "Why Are They Acting This Way?"

"We must not allow other people's limited perceptions to define us." —Virginia Satir

Satir's quote can be turned around to, "We must not let our limited perceptions define other people." Antipathy is often a byproduct of ignorance. If we're about to snap back at someone who's frustrating us, take a moment to realize their frustration may be a byproduct of our limited knowledge of their situation.

It's worth the time and effort to take a few seconds to ask yourself why they're behaving the way they are. Instead of putting them in their place, put yourself in their place. It can help you get past your initial antipathy and motivate you to respond proactively (instead of reactively), which in turn can motivate the other person to abandon their unpleasantness and treat you more courteously.

Tongue Fu! Tip for Teens

A high school student said, "I'm not buying this. Why should I let someone walk all over me?"

I'm not suggesting we let people walk all over us. I'm suggesting that we set a precedent for compassion—and that it's to our advantage to do so.

Did you ever stop to realize that when we make someone pay for their behavior, we pay right along with them? If I gave you a way to stop people from being obnoxious, wouldn't you want to try it?

In my workshops, I tell about the time my son and I went to our local ice cream store. The young woman behind the counter was doing her best to keep up with the crowd's requests for shakes and sundaes, but it was a hopeless cause. When it was finally our turn, I asked for three quarts of chocolate chip ice cream. The frazzled young woman put her hands on her hips and said in disbelief, "Three *quarts* of chocolate chip ice cream?! Do you know how *hard* it is to get that ice cream out of these containers?!"

Now, it might have been tempting to let loose a sarcastic, "*Well, excuuuse meee! I thought this was an ice cream store!*" However, that caustic remark wouldn't have helped. Instead, I asked myself, "Why would she say something like that?" Intuiting that she'd had a rough morning, I asked, "Has it been one of those kinds of days?"

Her rudeness melted away. She said with a big sigh, "Oh yes, I'm the only one here and it's been nonstop since I arrived. I was supposed to get off an hour ago, and the owner still hasn't come in." A few minutes later she sent us on our way with a friendly wave and a smile.

Do you see that empathizing is *not* about letting rude people walk all over us? It's about figuring out *why* people are being rude, which often gives us an insight into what we can say that will motivate them to stop being rude. By treating them in a friendly way, it makes it difficult for them to continue being difficult. Since we're seeing them as a person (not as a jerk), they start seeing us as a person (not as the source of their frustration).

Remember Tongue Fu! is about finessing, not fighting. Choosing to respond proactively (instead of reactively) has the power to turn initially unpleasant situations around, as it did with this young lady. That way, instead of everyone losing, everyone wins.

Action Plan for Fast-Forward through Frustration

Your basketball team is playing for the league championship. Unfortunately, demand for seats has exceeded supply. Even though the game isn't for another half hour, you have to close the doors and not let anyone else in because the gymnasium is already full. Many unhappy students and parents are locked out, and they're taking their frustration out on you. How do you handle it?

Words to Lose	Words to Use
You see things only from your point of view. *"Why are they blaming me? I'm only trying to enforce the fire codes."*	You see things from their point of view. *"I wish I could let them in. I know how much they want to see the game."*
You put them in their place. *"Well, you should have gotten here earlier. You knew this was a big game."*	You put yourself in their place. *"I can only imagine how frustrating this is for you."*
You feel put upon and the people get angrier because they feel you're unsympathetic. *"Listen up, there's nothing I can do about this. You're just going to have to accept the fact that you got here late."*	You feel empathetic and people don't take their anger out on you because they know you're doing your best. *"Please know if we could let you in, we would, and we need to honor the fire code."*

10

**"I personally think we developed language because of our deep inner
need to complain."**

—Lily Tomlin and Jane Wagner

Clear Up Complaints by Taking the AAA Train

Would you like to know what to do when people complain?
First, let's clarify what not to do. Don't explain!

We may think that if we explain why something didn't happen the
way it was supposed to, the other person will understand and forgive us.

Wrong. People perceive explanations as *excuses*. Explanations
make people angrier because they think we're not being accountable.

What to do instead? Take the AAA Train.

Ask Yourself, "Is What They're Saying Basically True?"

"Every great mistake has a halfway moment, a split second when
it can be recalled and perhaps remedied." —Pearl S. Buck

The next time someone complains, ask yourself, "Is what they're
saying basically true?"

Nine times out of ten, it is. That's why they're complaining. A commitment wasn't kept. A promise was broken. Instead of trying to explain why that agreement wasn't done *when* it was supposed to be done, or done the *way* it was supposed to be done, simply go to the heart of the matter with these two simple words, "You're right."

Those two words have an almost magical ability to defuse someone's anger. Complainers are upset because they feel they've been "betrayed." Instead of us (as the guilty party) going on and on about *how and why* they were betrayed, simply *acknowledge* the fact that the promise was broken, *apologize* for it, and then immediately set about taking *action* to fulfill the original promise. That way, you're correcting what went wrong instead of trying to justify it.

A teacher said this method worked a "mini-miracle" for her. She told me, "I had scheduled a parent/teacher conference with the parents of one of my students. Jeff was a bright young man; however, he spent far more time socializing than studying. He was more interested in goofing off than getting a good grade. His parents had agreed to meet me at 3:30 P.M. on a Thursday afternoon to discuss his performance in my class.

"Unfortunately, shortly after lunch that day, the flu bug that had been going around got me. I went from being fine to being violently ill in about twenty minutes. I dragged myself by the office on my way home, and asked the school secretary to get in touch with Jeff's parents, and ask if we could reschedule. That message never got to them. They waited outside my classroom for over an hour, thinking maybe I had gotten held up. They finally left, believing I'd forgotten our appointment. As you can imagine, they were not happy campers.

"Jeff's father called me at home to let me know, in no uncertain terms, how upset he was. I tried to tell him the school secretary was supposed to contact them and explain what happened, which made things even worse. The father said, 'So now you're trying to put this on someone else.'

"In the middle of this, I remembered the AAA Train and said, 'You're right.' I continued, 'Mr. Morales, I should have taken responsibility for getting in touch with you, and I'm sorry you and your wife went to the effort to get off work, waited so long, and I wasn't there. Please accept my apology. Can we either talk over the phone about Jeff's school performance or would you like to reschedule—and I promise to be there this time.'

"Just like that, it was over," the teacher said. "In retrospect, I realize that's all he wanted. Simply for me to admit that what happened was frustrating, that it shouldn't have happened, and that a sincere apology was due. As soon as I gave him that sincere apology, he was ready to move on."

Agree, Apologize, Act

"Good manners are made of petty sacrifices."
—Ralph Waldo Emerson

You may be thinking, "Why should I apologize if I didn't do anything wrong?"

Excellent question. The reason is if we didn't, people would stay mad at us, and who wants that? It's to our benefit to apologize even if we're not to blame because doing so is simply a way of commiserating with the other person's inconvenience.

The teacher wasn't to blame for the parents not being informed. If she had refused to apologize because "it wasn't her fault," Jeff's father would have continued to rail at her. She was simply putting herself in their shoes and imagining what it was like to go to all that trouble, stand in a hallway with no chairs, and wonder what the heck had happened. She imagined them waiting as twenty, thirty, forty-five minutes went by, and finally concluding she had irresponsibly forgotten the meeting.

When she saw the situation from their point of view, she realized that the truth of the matter was an agreement hadn't been kept. Whether or not it was her fault was beside the point. Jeff's parents were due an apology. So she made a "petty sacrifice" and gave it to them. And as soon as they received it, they were able to let go of their justifiable anger and move on.

We Can Be Right, or We Can Be Happy

"Don't make excuses, make good." —Frank Hubbard

Please understand that the root of many conflicts is that *something* has gone wrong, and neither party is willing to apologize because *they* didn't do anything wrong. Back and forth they go, each bound and determined to give their side of the issue, refusing to budge off the "rightness" of their perspective.

This is a prescription for a conflict. They may both be right, but their insistence on being right will make them both unhappy. If one person is "big" enough, as the teacher was, to offer an apology, it sets a precedent for civility. It brings the other person up to a more magnanimous level. Next time someone's complaining, and nothing you're saying is "getting through," it's probably because you're trying to explain the situation and that's not what the other person wants.

What they want is your expressed regret that something went wrong. If you say those magic words, "You're right," they will often, finally, get off their soapbox and be willing to discuss what can be done about the situation now.

The Express AA Train

"It takes less time to do something right than to explain why it was done wrong." —Henry Wadsworth Longfellow

There are exceptions to this (aren't there always?) statement. In today's litigious society, there are times we need to be careful about agreeing if it will open us up to liability. You know what we call that? Tongue Sue! No one wants Tongue Sue!

A situation with a school nurse demonstrates that there are times it can be counterproductive to say, "You're right." The nurse was called to the playground because a young girl had fallen off some playground equipment. The nurse examined the fifth grader, who initially seemed to be only bruised and shaken up. After giving her a few minutes to collect herself, the nurse helped her to her feet and they started to slowly walk to the health office. They had only gone a few feet when the girl cried out in pain and sunk to the ground, holding her leg, which was now bulging with what looked like a fracture.

The nurse, realizing the girl's injuries were more serious than she first thought, asked a fellow teacher on the playground to call an ambulance and to notify the parents.

It turned out the student did have a broken bone that had probably been cracked in the fall, then displaced when she put weight on it while walking. After the student was put in a cast at the hospital and taken home, the upset mother called the nurse and accused her of making the injury worse, "You should have known better than to get her up on her feet. You're incompetent."

Obviously, it would not be appropriate for the nurse to say, "You're right." Neither would it have helped to try to explain her actions, "Mrs. Solter, I asked your daughter if she felt anything was broken and she said no. When I examined Sue's leg, it was tender but there was no indication of any broken bones. I asked her if she could walk, and she said she thought so." This explanation would only have made the girl's mother angrier and she would have come back with, "She's a ten-year-old girl. You're supposed to be the expert." Do you see how explaining would have just perpetuated and escalated the conflict?

In that case, it's better to take the Express AA Train, *acknowledge* and *act*. "Mrs. Solter, I am so sorry to hear Sue's leg is broken. What can I do to help? Can I collect her belongings here at school and bring them to you? Can I contact her teachers and let them know the situation? Please tell me how I can support you and Sue."

Will the Express AA Train clear up any and all complaints? Nope. It will at least not exacerbate them, which is sometimes the best we can hope for. Remember, we can't always change the facts, but we can change the way we communicate and respond to the facts, which can change the way the other person chooses to respond to us.

Tongue Fu! Tip for Teens

A teenager in a workshop told me he was tired of teachers getting on his case all the time for being disorganized. I asked, "What do you mean?" He said, "Like today, I didn't turn in my essay for English. The thing was, I'd written it, I just forgot it at home. I kept trying to tell my teacher, but she wouldn't listen to me. She just kept saying, 'You're hurting yourself by not turning in papers when they're due. You've got to get better organized.'"

"Hmmm," I said, "Ron, is what your teacher saying true? Is it true that you're hurting yourself by not turning in your assignments on time? Is it true that it would help if you were better organized?"

"Yeah," he grudgingly admitted, "it is."

"Then why not just say that? Instead of trying to explain why you didn't turn your assignment in on time, just take the AAA Train. Say, 'You're right, Mrs. Lynch, the essay was due today, and I'm sorry I didn't bring it. I will bring it in tomorrow, and from now on I'll check to make sure I have the right books and papers before I leave the house.'

"*That's* what she wants to hear, not an explanation of why you don't have your homework with you. Plus, it moves you from thinking 'she won't listen to me' to realizing she has a valid point and it's up to you to do something to change the situation instead of complaining she's getting on your case."

Action Plan for Clear Up Complaints by Taking the AAA Train

There are not enough classrooms at your school and several trailers were supposed to be installed over the summer to accommodate the extra students. Unfortunately, construction wasn't completed by the start of the school year, and several classes have to be combined until the trailers are ready. The teachers are up in arms about this situation. As the principal, what do you do?

Words to Lose	Words to Use
You tell them what went wrong and why. *"The work crews got behind because of all the summer rains."*	You ask yourself, "Is what they're saying basically true?" *"You're right, the trailers were supposed to be ready by September 3."*
You belabor the explanation and it heightens the conflict. *"Hey, this place was a mud bowl. It was impossible for them to stay on schedule."*	You bypass the explanation and it lessens the conflict. *"I know you were looking forward to having your own classrooms."*
You feel helpless that they're complaining about something you can't do anything about. *"Hey, it's out of my hands. There's nothing we can do but wait until they're ready to move into."*	You understand how helpless they feel and acknowledge their feelings. *"I can only imagine how frustrating it is being squeezed in together."*

Words to Lose	Words to Use
You refuse to apologize because it's not your fault, which perpetuates the tension and conflict. *"You're just going to have to make the best of it. They're working as hard as they can, and complaining about it isn't going to speed things up."*	You make a "petty sacrifice" and take the AAA Train to set a precedent for civility. *"I'm sorry the trailers aren't ready for you. I'm going to talk with the foreman today to see if there's any way they can get these ready sooner."*

11

"One friend, one person who is truly understanding, who takes the trouble to listen to us as we consider our problems, can change our whole outlook on the world."

—Elton Mayo

Listen Up!

Who is someone who *really* listens to you? What do they do that makes them such a good listener? How do they make you feel? How do you feel about them? I've asked this question at every Tongue Fu! program in the last ten years, and an astonishing trend has emerged. Most of us know hundreds of people, yet we can probably only think of one or two people who *really* listen to us. It's that rare.

As Mayo pointed out above, when we *really* listen to people, it has the power to change their whole outlook on the world. What we may not realize is that it also has the power to change *our* outlook on the world.

As covered in chapter 9, listening means temporarily putting our own opinions aside and taking on board the other person's perceptions. You probably agree with the importance of this, but you might be thinking, "How can I do that? Most of the time, I'm so busy I hardly have time to listen to myself. It's not that I don't want to listen, it's just that at school I have students, meetings, and faculty responsibilities competing for my attention, and at home I have chores, paperwork, and family members competing for my attention."

Are You Giving Partial Attention or Patient Attention?

"If I have made any valuable discoveries, it has been owing more
to patient attention than to any other talent." —Sir Isaac Newton

An example of this "perpetual preoccupation" was demonstrated at
the dinner table one night when my sons and I were discussing weekend plans. We were deciding what to do when I noticed Tom looked a little distracted. I asked, "Tom, are you listening to me?"

"Sure Mom," he replied, "You've got my *undevoted* attention." Out
of the mouths of teens!

With so much competing for our attention, it's easy to give fellow
faculty members, students, parents, and administrators our *undevoted* attention. However, there are times when we sense someone
needs our *undivided* attention. These next four "Give 'Em 'L'" steps
can help us give someone our full, patient attention even when we have
lots on our mind.

Look the other person in the eyes

M. Scott Peck says, "You cannot truly listen to anyone and do anything
else at the same time." Our attention is where our eyes are. If our eyes
are moving around or focused elsewhere, people will think we're distracted and will either shut down or escalate their behavior in an effort
to get our full attention. They won't believe we're focused on them until
we look at their face.

Lean toward them

If you're working on your computer or facing the chalkboard, people will
conclude you're only "half-listening" because you're obviously otherwise
occupied. Place your papers and pen on the desk, or turn away from what
you're working on. These body movements say, "This can wait. You are
more important." Such actions on your part indicate, both physically and
psychologically, that this person is your top priority. Furthermore, when
you lean toward someone, you are literally and figuratively reaching out
to that person. Your "edge of the seat" posture indicates that you're interested in what they have to say and will motivate them to confide in you.

Lift your eyebrows

Try this. It works. If your face is slack, your interest will be slack. Even if you're exhausted, the mere act of lifting your eyebrows animates your face, eliminates lethargy, and activates interest. By lifting your eyebrows, you both appear more interested and *feel* more interested.

Get on their level

If you are dealing with young people, it's imperative to hunker down on their level so you can (once again, literally and figuratively) see things eye to eye. No matter how empathic you are, if they are 3½ feet tall, and you are 5½ feet tall, there's too big of a gap in your perspectives. They'll never really believe you understand things from their point of view—because you're not at their point of view! Only when you lean over so your face is at their level—or sit down so you're eye to eye—will they truly believe you know how they feel.

Are We Really Listening or Are We Waiting for Our Turn to Talk?

> "Conversation in the United States is a competitive exercise in which the first person to draw a breath is considered the listener." —Nathan Miller

Most anger is a cry for attention. If people are upset and feel they're not getting their urgent message across to us, they will escalate their behavior to force us to pay attention. By giving people 'L,' we can either 1) prevent them from becoming argumentative in the first place because they'll have what they want—our ears, or 2) they'll lower their voice and become more rational because they no longer have to resort to histrionics to get us to notice them.

Yet putting our thoughts on hold can be difficult when we feel something so intensely we can't wait to express it. It can feel like the other person is getting in the way of what we want to say. Naval aviators call this urge to express what's on our mind being "stuck on transmit." It's technically impossible for pilots to send and receive a radio transmission at the same time. They must talk, then listen. It makes talking and listening mutually exclusive. We can't do both at the same time; we have to do one, then the other, one, then the other.

How can we train ourselves to listen when all we really want to do is transmit? First, when we're impatient to burst out with what's on the tip of our tongue, we can ask ourselves, "Am I really listening or am I waiting for my turn to talk?" If we're just waiting for them to put a sock in it so we can share our opinions, we can remind ourselves to Look, Lean, Lift, and get on their Level. That will help us focus more on what they have to say and less on what we want to say.

Second, we can picture this visual image of a two-way radio to help us discipline ourselves to listen and then talk, listen and then talk. The word "listen" has the same letters as the word "silent" for good reason. Picture yourself pressing an over-and-out button when you finish talking and then giving your mind over to their incoming message. Silently absorb every word. Instead of formulating your own opinions about the validity of their remarks, ask yourself, "How would I feel if this were happening to me?" That empathy phrase will help you focus on their perspective instead of your own. Only after the other person has signed off, do you sign on and respond to what's been said.

Listen to Uncover What's Really Going On

> "Listening means taking a vigorous, human interest in what is being told us. You can listen like a blank wall or like a splendid auditorium where every sound comes back fuller and richer."
> —Alice Dyer Miller

A woman who was alumni chair and in charge of her twenty-fifth high school reunion said she was grateful for this idea because it kept her from making an embarrassing faux pas. Tess told me, "I had assigned the different responsibilities to the eight people on our planning committee, and had scheduled our first conference call to get updates."

"The day of our call, I started getting e-mails from people saying they didn't have their status reports ready. I was furious. I couldn't believe how irresponsible these people were being. When we started the call, I was fully prepared to read them the riot act. Then, our food & beverage chair apologized for not having her report ready and explained that, just that week, she'd had to put her parents in an assisted living facility. They were understandably unhappy about having to leave their home of fifty years, and it had been a heartbreaking experience for everyone.

"Then, another committee member spoke up to say she usually kept her commitments but was going through chemotherapy and had been too exhausted to do much of anything but lay in bed. One by one, they each described some extraordinary circumstances that had taken higher priority in the prior weeks."

Tess said, "I was so glad I listened to them instead of barging ahead with my 'riot act' remarks. As soon as I found out what they'd been going through, it put things in instant perspective. All of a sudden, whether to get an oldies band or a DJ for our twenty-fifth reunion wasn't nearly so important."

Learn to Listen, Listen to Learn

"If you're not listening, you're not learning." —Lyndon B. Johnson

An administrator told me, "I've always prided myself on my open door policy. I didn't realize until you covered these 'Give 'Em "L"' and two-way radio ideas that my door may be open; however, my mind is often closed.

"When people walk in to talk to me, I'm often in the middle of something. Without really meaning to, I treat them as an unwelcome interruption. I'll glance up from my computer and say rather distractedly, 'Yes?' I can see now that my split attention sends the message that, 'You're bothering me. Hurry up so I can get back to work.'

"When I get back to the office, I'm going to schedule a Listening Hour in the afternoon between 3 and 4 P.M. During that designated hour, I'll put other things aside and make sure people who want or need to talk with me feel their concerns are my first priority."

I complimented this manager for vowing to be more mindful of her staff and told her about a survey that asked employees from a variety of industries this one question: "Do you like your boss?" The results were surprising. Respondents who replied, "Yes, I like my boss," said the number one reason why was, "He/she listens to me." Guess what the most frequently given reason was for not liking your boss? "He/she doesn't listen to me."

Giving people our undivided attention is the single best way we can make them feel significant. In essence, we're saying, "You're the most important thing in my world right now. I could be doing any number of things; however, I'm choosing to give you my complete attention." It is a gift.

This wise manager understood if she didn't set aside time to listen to people, they would soon feel ignored, morale would suffer, and crucial issues would go unaddressed. She also intuited that if people came to her upset and she didn't concentrate on what they were saying, she would miss important clues that could help turn around the situation. She was smart to welcome them with "open ears" so she could learn what was working, what wasn't, and what she could do to correct it. By paying attention up front, she won't have to spend extra time trying to resolve situations that escalated because she didn't invest the necessary listening time at the outset.

Preclude Preoccupation

"If we don't have time to do it right the first time, when are we going to have time to do it over again?" —office poster

Who is someone who is overdue for some listening from you? Could you have unintentionally been shutting this person down because she or he sensed you were preoccupied? Is there a certain student, teacher, or family member who has received more than their share of "Not now," "Catch you later," or "Keep it short"?

When will you see this person next? Could you vow right now that the next time you see them, you will stop what you're doing, get on their level, look them in the eye, and lean forward so they know you really want to hear what they have to say? Could you mentally put everything else on hold for a minimum of three to five minutes and give them your complete concentration? Giving your undivided attention is an eloquent way of saying "I value you," and can compensate for other times you've been physically present but mentally elsewhere.

Are you thinking, "What if the next time I see this person, I've got other responsibilities and I'm not in a position to make them my top priority?" Then make eye contact with them so they "get" your sincerity and tell them, "I really want to hear what you have to say. And I know it seems we've been like two ships passing in the night. Please know I want to get together, and right now I've got to take care of _____ [fill in the blank]. Could we set up a time later today for us to connect?" People will understand that you have other obligations; what they won't understand or forgive is when you're perennially too busy to talk or listen to them.

Karl Menninger said, "Listening is a magnetic thing, a creative force. The people who listen to us are the ones we move toward, and we want to sit in their radius. When we are listened to, it creates us, makes us unfold and expand."

Part of educating is helping students unfold and expand. Commit to becoming a better listener and it will benefit everyone fortunate enough to sit in your radius.

Tongue Fu! Tip for Teens

When I interviewed teens and asked what they would ask of teachers if they could, their number one request was, "Please listen to me."

My niece Christy said, "My geometry teacher was explaining this new concept and I was right on the verge of understanding it. He showed us how to work a problem and then asked if there were any questions. I raised my hand, but I couldn't figure how to phrase what was scrambling around in my mind. He interrupted and finished my sentence for me. It wasn't what I wanted to say, but he moved on before I could figure out how to say it. That happens a lot.

"I know teachers are rushed, that some of them have taught the same subject year after year, and they've heard the same questions hundreds of times before; however, I wish they'd be a little more patient and let us get things out instead of cutting us off and assuming they know what we were going to ask."

I said, "Christy, that's an interesting observation. What do you think you could do if you're trying to articulate something that's not quite formed yet and a teacher doesn't give you time to crystallize your thoughts?"

She said with a grin, "I'd say, 'Please give me a chance. I think I'm on the verge of something original here. . . . I just need a few more seconds to get it out.'"

Sounds like a good plan to me. How about to you?

Action Plan for Listen Up!

You stay in your classroom during lunch to get caught up on paperwork. Ten minutes into lunch, a student stops by and asks to talk with you. She's just broken up with her boyfriend and she's crying. Your heart goes out to her, but you need to turn in these forms by the end of the day. What do you do?

Words to Lose	Words to Use
You think only of your own responsibilities and tell her you can't talk right now. *"Emily, I can't talk to you right now. I have to get these papers done."*	You think of her needs and give her five minutes of your time. *"Sure Emily, I've got a few minutes. Come on in."*
You get impatient because she's keeping you from your other work. *You think to yourself, "This is the last thing I need right now."*	You give your undivided attention so she knows she's important. *"Let me put these papers aside. Tell me what's happening."*
You half listen and she feels shut down and that you don't really care. *"Uh, what was that again? I'm sorry, I missed that."*	You give her 'L' to preclude preoccupation and to stay focused. *"So, he said he wants to date other girls?"*
You don't really hear what she's saying and she leaves more upset than when she walked in. *"You'll get over him. This happens to all of us, one time or another."*	You diplomatically ask if you can talk again later to go in more depth. *"I've got time after school. Want to come back in and we'll talk about this some more?"*

12

"It has always surprised me how little attention philosophers have paid to humor since it is a more significant process of mind than reason. Reason can only sort out perceptions, but the humor process is involved in changing them."

—Edward de Bono

Use Fun Fu! to Handle Hassles with Humor

Are you ready to lighten up? After discussing conflicts, rudeness, and complaints, you may be ready for some comic relief—which is the point of this chapter. A little humor can go a long way to easing tension. It may be just what we need to stop taking the situation and ourselves so seriously.

One of my favorite examples of Fun Fu! took place in an airport. I was riding a moving sidewalk down one of the long hallways when I noticed a very tall man walking toward me. I couldn't believe it. Several people in front of me were pointing at him and laughing. I thought "How rude!" and then he got closer and I could see why they were laughing. He had on a T-shirt that said in big letters, "*No, I'm NOT a basketball player.*"

I turned to compliment him as he walked by and started laughing out loud. The back of his shirt said, "*Are you a jockey?*" This was too good to let pass. I ran back to catch up with him and asked, "Where did you get that terrific shirt?"

He smiled and said, "My mom made 'em for me." He went on to explain, "I grew a foot between the time I was sixteen and eighteen years old. I didn't even want to go outside because everyone had to make a smart aleck remark. My mom finally told me, 'If you can't beat 'em, join 'em.'"

He continued, "This is nothing. I've got a whole drawer full of these at home. My favorite says, 'I'm 6-foot 13-inches and the weather up here's fine.' Then he closed with the clincher. "Ever since I started wearing these shirts, I've had fun with my height instead of being frustrated by my height." A smart young man.

Is there something you're sensitive about? If you're short, tall, fat, skinny, or losing your hair, you're going to hear about it. Why not come up with a repertoire of clever, noncombative comebacks so people no longer have the power to push your hot buttons? Like this young man discovered, if you have an issue that isn't going to "go away," (i.e., your height) you have a choice. You can continue to be annoyed or rattled when people comment on it, or you can come up with some responses to handle their remarks with poise rather than panic.

What Are Your Hot Buttons?

"Perhaps one has to become very old before one learns to be amused, rather than offended." —Pearl S. Buck

There was a marvelous episode of the TV sitcom "Mad about You" where Helen Hunt's character was preparing for a visit from her perfectionist mom. She spent the entire day cleaning the house, cooking an elaborate meal, and making everything just so. Then her mother showed up and nothing was good enough. She became more and more dejected as her mom found fault with everything in sight. She turned to her husband and muttered, "My mother is a travel agent for guilt trips." After a thoroughly discouraging evening, they finally went to bed. Helen turned to her husband and said, "I don't get it. I'm thirty-five years old. Why is it my mother can still push all my hot buttons?"

"That's easy," he said. "She installed them."

Actually, we install our own hot buttons. People do not have the power to push our buttons unless we give them that power. Taunts can fall on deaf ears if we choose to be amused rather than offended.

People's attempts to knock us off balance won't work if we have a sense of humor about our shortcomings instead of being defensive about our shortcomings.

What Are You Sensitive About?

"If we can laugh at it, we can live with it." —Erma Bombeck

"This idea was a confidence-saver for me," one woman said. "Some friends suggested I run for our county school board. I had raised five children who had all gone through the public school system and I had been very active in their activities. I had never had political aspirations, but I was fed up with the lousy condition of our schools and the fact that no one seemed to be doing anything about it. These parents said that when I had been president of the elementary, junior, and senior high school PTAs, those had been the best years those schools had ever seen—and they would actively support my campaign if I would run. I was suffering a little from empty nest syndrome at the time and decided 'Why not?'

"One thing I was concerned about was I hadn't graduated from college. I got married my second year in college and got pregnant my third, and never went back. I was sure this was going to come up, and I was afraid the other candidates would make a big deal about it. Sure enough, one of my opponents brought it up at our first public debate. He said self-righteously, 'I think it's important for school board representatives to have academic backgrounds so they're familiar with the issues they'll be deciding.' He went on with, 'I have a Master's in Education from [and he named a respected university].' He then turned to me and asked pointedly, 'And what type of degree do you have, Marilynn?'

"Thankfully, my campaign manager and I had anticipated this and had prepared an answer. 'I have a 5K Degree,' I said with a warm, relaxed smile.

"Puzzled, he asked, 'A 5K Degree. What's that?'

"A Five Kid Degree. In the last twenty-five years, I've raised five children who attended and graduated from our local schools, and I am well aware of the issues facing our educational system.' The audience applauded and my lack of a college degree became a nonissue."

Bravo. Instead of allowing him to turn this issue into a source of embarrassment, she turned it into an asset. That's the power of Fun Fu!

Learn to Laugh at Life

"I learned quickly that when I made others laugh, they liked me.
This lesson I will never forget." —Art Buchwald

A fellow speaker from California tells a wonderful story which further illustrates the benefits of choosing to handle hassles with a chuckle rather than a curse.

Jim Pelley, www.LaughterWorkers.com, gave me permission to share his story because he too believes it's in our best interests to laugh at life rather than lament over it. Jim was on a packed flight, seated next to the original Difficult Person. His seatmate was one of the last passengers to board. All the overhead bins were full so he had to check his carry-on. He was in the middle seat in the middle row; there was a crying baby in front of him, and a toddler behind him who kept playing with the tray table. Suffice it to say, this guy was not a happy camper.

On top of that, it took almost two hours to serve the meal and when it arrived, it was a cold snack instead of a hot entrée. The disgruntled passenger took one bite out of his sandwich, slammed it back down on his plate, and jammed his finger on the flight attendant call button.

The flight attendant came over and asked, "Yes sir, how can I help you?"

He shoved the sandwich in her outstretched hand and snarled, "This sandwich is bad."

A little taken aback, she looked at him and looked at the sandwich. Looked at him again, looked back at the sandwich.

Looked at him . . . and then shook her finger at the snack and said, "*Bad* sandwich, *bad* sandwich."

Deer in headlights. After a moment of shock, they both burst out laughing and the guy was cooperative for the rest of the trip.

Jim wanted to meet this Fun Fu! Black Belt in person, so later in the flight he went back to the galley and mimicked what had happened, "Bad sandwich, bad sandwich. That was brilliant," he said, "Did you just think of that?!"

She smiled and said, "I've been a flight attendant for twenty-five years. I learned a long time ago that there was going to be at least one difficult person on every flight, and I better learn how to turn him around. If I didn't, he was going to ruin my flight and the flight of everyone around him."

"So, what'd you do?" Jim asked.

"I went to all the stews (that's what we called ourselves back then) and asked 'What if?' questions. *What if* we have a mechanical and have to head back to the terminal? *What if* we're seventeenth in line to take off and everyone's going to miss their connection?" She said, "I have a whole repertoire of things to say so no matter what goes wrong, I can get on the intercom and defuse it."

Jim asked, "What's an example?"

She said, "If we run out of chicken and all we have left is Salisbury steak, I'll make the announcement and then say, 'And no, to answer your question, the Salisbury steak can NOT be used as a flotation device.' We have upwards of three hundred people on some of our larger flights. When we're delayed for some reason, the mood on the plane can get downright ugly. It's not that these announcements are hilarious or anything, it's just the fact that the humor is unexpected and it cuts the tension like a knife. It helps passengers see us as human beings instead of these faceless airline employees and they stop taking their anger out on us."

Humor Helps Us Be More Humane

"Humor is the great thing, the saving thing, after all. The minute it crops up, our irritations and resentments flit away, and a sunny spirit takes their place." —Mark Twain

That's yet another benefit of humor. When we're upset, we often take our frustration out on the messenger. We don't see that person as a fellow human being who's a mother, father, brother, sister—just like us. Instead, we see them as an employee or representative of an organization we're mad at. When that person uses appropriate humor it humanizes them, and we're less likely to continue treating them inhumanely.

Keith Adey, a certified Tongue Fu! trainer in Newfoundland, told me about a first year teacher who was having difficulty with classroom management. The principal overheard him reading the riot act to the class every day. It seemed the more the teacher yelled at the class, the more they misbehaved. He was ordering students, "Sit in your seats, take out your books, stop talking, and look at me."

The principal tried to help this young man because he felt he wasn't going to make it as a teacher if he did not change his approach. The principal paired him up with a mentor, another teacher on staff, and part of the mentoring experience included team teaching. This gave the new teacher a chance to observe a more experienced veteran in action.

After a couple of weeks the principal noticed there was hardly any yelling in the new teacher's class. There also seemed to be less noise from the students. The principal called the novice teacher into his office and asked him how the mentoring was going. The young man said he realized he was screaming *at* his students instead of talking *with* his students. He said, "When I stay calm, I get more respect." The teacher also said when he makes a request (in a friendly tone) of the students such as, "Would you take out your books and get ready for class?" students tended to comply more.

And here was the clincher. The teacher now starts each morning with a joke. He combs newspapers, magazines, and the "funny papers" for something that makes him laugh out loud and then shares it with the class. And he lets students share theirs (as long as the jokes are clean). He said the students are beginning to have fun in his class and he is beginning to enjoy teaching.

Don't Forget to Have Fun

"Humor is just another defense against the universe."
—Mel Brooks

A friend and teacher read this manuscript to give me feedback and laughed when she read this page, "Oh yeah," she said, "That's right. Teaching's supposed to be fun."

With all of the pressures in education these days, it can be easy to lose sight of the fact that children are full of humor. Kids really do say the darnedest things. Take a tip from a group of IRS auditors and put up a bulletin board with all the funny things your students say. Post all the jokes, cartoons, and one-liners you can find about anything to do with your topic, school, or profession. Your "wall of wit" can be a defense against the trials and tribulations that sometimes come with the teaching territory.

How does this work? Well, a group of IRS auditors who participated in a Tongue Fu! workshop decided to put up their own Wall of Wit. No one likes to be audited. However, the auditors were hoping to counteract the antagonism they faced on a daily basis. One auditor told me, "Just about everyone who walks in our door sees us as the enemy. So we've filled a bulletin board in our lobby with jokes about the IRS, or Income Removal Service as we call it now. One of my favorites says in big bold letters, 'The secret is stop thinking of it as your money!' When taxpayers read our welcoming sign that says, 'Sorry, we're in!' they soften a little and start seeing us as human beings."

What's your hot button? Is there a comment or question that knocks you off balance? Could you brainstorm Fun Fu! responses so you need never be tongue-tied again? Once people realize you're not self-conscious about the topic, and once you demonstrate you can poke fun at yourself, they'll stop poking fun at you.

Tongue Fu! Tip for Teens

In an ideal world, we would all be kind, compassionate human beings all the time. Unfortunately, that's more optimistic than realistic. Like it or not, life in school is often a nonstop pecking order with kids taunting you to see "what you're made of." If you give as good as you get, they'll often choose to leave you alone because you're "up to their test."

I am not suggesting you go around ridiculing classmates to prove your superiority. I am suggesting that, if you're being teased about something, it's in your best interests to come up with a Fun Fu! response, fast. If you're self-concious about your size, acne, clothes, ethnicity, ANYTHING, you will be a target. The sooner you shrug off their comments, the sooner they'll leave you alone.

With a last name like Horn, you can imagine the kidding my two sons received. When you're ten and being called "Horny" all the time, it gets old fast. After brainstorming this over dinner one night, the boys came up with a comeback. From then on, if someone started giving them a hard time about their name, they'd say, "That's my name, *please* wear it out." That retort may not be side-splittingly funny, but it was better than stammering, blushing, or getting mad, all rewarding overreactions that delighted teasers by letting them know their jab had worked.

It might help to see taunts as bait. The teaser is hoping you'll get angry, which is proof he or she "hooked" you. By tossing back a humorous remark, you've refused to "bite," and they'll respect you for not losing your cool. We'll talk more about teasing, especially teasing that crosses over into bullying, in chapter 26, "Break Free from Bullies."

Action Plan for Use Fun Fu! to Handle Hassles with Humor

An attractive teacher in her late twenties told me she was tired of all the comments she receives about her appearance and choice of profession. "Every time I go out and guys find out what I do, they say stuff like, 'What's a fine-looking woman like you doing in a job like that?' I take teaching seriously and it bothers me when people disrespect me and my work. What would you do?"

Words to Lose	Words to Use
You let people push your hot buttons.	You prepare answers for your hot buttons.
"If one more person implies that teaching is a second-class profession, I'm going to lose it."	*"So, you think all teachers should wear white sweaters, glasses, and look like Mrs. Doubtfire?"*
You get frustrated by people's insensitive remarks.	You have fun with people's remarks.
"I can't believe you just said, 'Why isn't a cute young thing like you married?!'"	*"Let's just put it this way. I think, therefore I'm single."*
You handle hassles with harsh words.	You handle hassles with humor.
"Quit giving me advice I didn't ask for. Why don't you get lost, jerk?"	*"When I want your opinion, I'll give it to you."*
You add to the tension by getting upset.	You ease the tension by choosing to be amused.
"Oh grow up. My teenaged students have better manners than you do."	*"Didn't your mama teach you better manners than that?"*

"Anyone who doesn't think there are two sides to an argument is probably in one!"

—Tongue Fu'ism

Focus on Solutions, Not Fault

Would you like to know what to do if a discussion has deteriorated into faultfinding and finger-pointing? Stop it with the following hand gesture.

No, no not that one!

Hold your hand up like a police officer would. Why does this bring hostilities to a halt? It's a universally understood signal to cease and desist. If you try to talk over people who are arguing, what will they do? That's right, they'll talk louder. Your voice of reason will get drowned out in the commotion. If you hold your hand up, fingers toward the sky and palm out, people will stop quarrelling for just a moment, which gives you time to get your verbal foot in the door and say these argument-ending words, "*We're here to find solutions, not faults.*"

Arguments Serve No Good Purpose

"I never saw an instance of two disputants convincing the other by argument." –Thomas Jefferson

In almost every controversy, each person has legitimate points. It's not that one side is true and the other is false, both sides usually have valid views. As long as each side insists on trying to prove the rightness of their point of view, the two will remain in a dispute.

The point of this chapter is that it is often point*less* to go back and forth trying to figure out who is at fault, because that won't correct the problem. A far better use of time is to figure out what can be done about the situation, rather than trying to affix blame for who's responsible for the situation.

This was illustrated by a principal who returned home from a conference expecting to find SOL (Standard of Learning) progress reports on his desk, only to find the teachers didn't know anything about his request. He convened a staff meeting to "get to the bottom of this." The teachers claimed they hadn't been told of his request. He turned to Alice, his assistant, and said heatedly, "I gave you explicit directions to send out a memo asking for these reports." She defended herself with, "I did write the memo. I gave it to Clarice to copy and send out." Clarice, in shock, said, "What memo?" Alice replied, "I put it on your desk last Monday." Clarice said, "Well, I never saw it." Alice came back with, "Well, if you would clean your desk every once in awhile, you might be able to find things."

At this point, the principal intervened by putting his hand up and saying, "This won't help. We could spend the rest of the afternoon arguing about who put what where, and it won't get these SOL reports done. Instead, let's figure out how we can get these finished and turned in by noon Monday, and let's set up a system where we follow up on important memos to make sure they've been understood and acted on."

Bravo. He understood that debating who dropped the ball served no constructive purpose. Instead of bickering about who didn't do what they were supposed to do and why, it was better to turn their attention to how everyone could complete the required assignment and keep this oversight from reoccurring.

Turn Bickering into Brainstorming

"See problems as holes in the ground. You can dig deeper, or you can break new ground." —Anonymous

There's another way to halt hostilities. Make a T with your hand the way referees, coaches, and athletes do to call a time out, and then say, "Cut it out. Yelling at each other won't resolve this. Instead, let's focus on how we can keep this from happening again."

This is an effective way to stop people in the midst of a senseless squabble and move their attention from an accusing "Who did it?" frame of mind to an action-oriented "What can we do about it?" frame of mind. Instead of trying to ascertain who's responsible for the problem, start brainstorming how you can resolve the problem.

A program attendee used this technique with great results. She and her family had just returned from a two-week vacation. As soon as they walked into their house, they were met by a terrible smell. They started walking through the different rooms, trying to figure out where the smell was coming from. They went into the kitchen and found the refrigerator door wide open. All the food had spoiled. As Ann said, "The blaming began."

"Who was the last person in the house?" "Don't blame me. I didn't get in the refrigerator. You were the one who went back in to get a soda."

"In the middle of all this finger-pointing, I remembered your technique. I made a T and held it up in the air and shouted above the fray, 'Time out.' Then I said calmly, 'We could argue 'til the cows come home about who left the refrigerator door open, and it won't get this kitchen cleaned up. Instead, let's all pitch in and take care of this mess. When we're finished, let's come up with a plan so from now on when we leave for a trip, someone's in charge of going around and making sure everything is shut down and closed up.'"

We Can Fix the Blame or Fix the Situation

"Our task is not to fix the blame for the past, it's to fix the course for the future." —John F. Kennedy

A public official voiced some skepticism, "Normally I would agree with this; however, aren't there times we have to assess blame? We recently had an embarrassing financial scandal. If we don't indicate who is responsible for embezzling those funds, we'll all take the fall."

He's right. There are exceptions to this rule. For example, if you are a Board of Education administrator and someone on your team has been found guilty of an illegal act, it is important to address this issue and assert that this individual's actions were not condoned or associated with the rest of the group. Be sure to clarify that you are being forced to "point the finger" and it is not your normal style. You can say, "I wish I didn't have to do this because I prefer not to operate this way. However, these unfortunate circumstances demand that we name the person responsible for this unlawful behavior so he will be held accountable. Then, as a board, we want to focus on the steps we've taken to keep something like this from happening again so we can reestablish our reputation for integrity."

Don't Ask, "What Happened?"

"At the moment of truth, there are either reasons or results."
—Chuck Yeager, aviation pioneer

Glenda, my sons' wise preschool teacher, taught me that my well-intended efforts to intervene in their squabbles often had the unintended effect of reinforcing and rewarding them. How so? The more I tried to mediate their disagreements, the more I concentrated on their disagreements. For children who want attention, this flicks on a switch in their mind that says, "Hmm, mom is busy doing something else. Guess I'll make some trouble to get her attention."

What to do instead? Imagine you're a playground supervisor. Some first-graders are playing with a ball. The next thing you know one of them is crying. First, don't assume you know what happened. Second, don't ask, "What happened?" If you do, you'll just encourage "he said/she said" accusations. "He took the ball away from me." "Well, I had it first." "Did not." "Did so." Back and forth they'll go.

It's a no-win trying to figure out who started it because each child will have his or her own version of events. Unless you saw the incident yourself and know exactly what happened, refrain from trying to affix blame. Instead, separate the two children, hold your hand up, and ask them to "Make silence." Once they're both quiet, say, "Each of you will get your turn," then turn to one and ask, "What would you like to have happen now?" "I would like to have a turn with the ball." Turn to the other and ask, "What would you like to have happen?" "I would like to play with the ball."

Then say, "Okay, you both want to play with the ball. You have a choice. You can play together with the ball for the remainder of recess, or you can each have it for three minutes. Which do you want to do?" Whichever option they choose, wrap things up by saying, "Let me make this clear. As long as you play with the ball nicely, you can keep it. If there is any more fighting, the ball gets taken away and neither one of you gets to play with it. Now, what is our agreement?"

You may be thinking, "What if one of the children is a bully and the other child really was innocently playing when the bully wrestled the ball away?" In chapter 26, "Break Free from Bullies," we'll talk about what to do when a child has a history of taking advantage of others. For now, the point of this chapter is that it is healthier to help children focus on ways they can get along instead of allowing them to stay focused on the reasons why they're not getting along.

Inflexibility Never Helped Anyone

"The significant problems we face cannot be solved at the same level of thinking with which they were created." —Albert Einstein

A primary message of this chapter is that inflexibly clinging to our position torpedoes any chance of a win–win resolution. Someone needs to "take the high road" and choose to focus on how the situation can be resolved instead of trying to prove he or she is right.

A school orchestra conductor said this insight helped him resolve a situation that was about to turn ugly. He said, "I had reserved the school auditorium for 6 P.M. so we could rehearse for our holiday recital. I walked in about a quarter to six, only to find the drama club already there, holding auditions for the school play. I told the head of the theater department we had the auditorium reserved and he said rather testily, 'I don't see how you can have the auditorium reserved. Auditions were last night, tonight, and tomorrow night. Haven't you seen the signs around campus?'

"I showed him a copy of our confirmed reservation and he said, 'I've got one of those too.' I realized the office must have made a mistake and scheduled us both in the auditorium for the same night. I realized getting upset wasn't going to help anybody, so I suggested, 'Can we put our heads together and see if we can come up with a win–win solution to this? Is there any way you could end a half hour early and I'll tell my group we're going to start a half hour late? That way, this will work out for both of us.' He saw the sense of that and agreed."

What are you going to do next time something goes wrong? Instead of wasting everyone's time figuring out who's right and wrong, could you use that time instead to figure out how to resolve the situation? Someone's got to get creative and get past the blaming, shaming, and finger-pointing. Why not you?

Tongue Fu! Tip for Teens

What do you do if a couple of your friends are arguing , really getting into it? You may think, "I'll stay out of it." Could you instead act as a verbal traffic cop? You may be an "innocent bystander," however if your buddies are headed for a fight, intervening could help them from saying something they won't be able to take back.

Imagine one of your friends is still nursing a grudge because he wasn't included in a beach trip your pals took last summer. Justin says, "You could have fit one more person in the van." Dan comes back with, "I've told you a hundred times, my mom said I could only take three people." Justin protests, "I would have paid my own way. I could have slept on the floor." Dan rolls his eyes in exasperation, "You're not listening. It wasn't about the money. My mom said. . . . "

Motivate your friends to close the books on this issue and put it behind them. Make a T with your hands to get their attention and say, "Hey, once and for all, give it a rest. It's time to put that in the past and move on."

If they start in again, interrupt and say, "Let it go" or "It's over. Let's talk about something else." If Justin brings it up again, don't let him get started. Use his name (because people pause for just a second when you say their name), "It's history. Onward." You're doing everyone a favor by refusing to let them wrangle about something that happened months ago.

Notice, don't use the word "you." Saying, "You guys cut it out," or "You guys are driving me crazy" would escalate the situation because it would seem like you were scolding them with a "holier than thou" attitude. By using the word "we're" or "let's," you're including yourself in the mix instead of preaching. They'll be able to hear what you're saying without being offended because it'll be clear you're acting in everyone's best interests.

Action Plan for Focus on Solutions, Not Fault

You walk into the teachers' lounge and two teachers are arguing. Your "open" school has no doors on the classrooms. It seems one teacher has accused her neighbor of being so noisy the students in her own class can't concentrate. The other teacher is insulted and this has now escalated into a brouhaha. What do you do?

Words to Lose	Words to Use
You decide to stay out of it. This isn't your battle. *"I'm grabbing my cup of coffee and I'm out of here."*	You decide to play traffic cop to end the argument. *"Somebody needs to intervene or else this will get worse."*
You try to talk over them and they get louder. *"Hey you two, you're making such a racket, you can hear it in the halls."*	You use a hand signal to get their attention. *"Time out. Calling each other names won't help."*
You ask them to explain what's going on which keeps them focused on who's at fault. *"What's happening? Why are you shouting at each other?"*	You ask them what they want, which helps them focus on the future. *"What can we do to honor each other's need for quiet?"*
You use the word "you," which makes them feel like you're chastising them. *"You two need to stop this. You're acting like children."*	You use the words "let's" and "we" so they know you're acting in the best interests of the group. *"Let's agree to notify each other when our students are taking a test so our neighboring teacher can keep the sound down."*

14

"There is nothing wrong with people that reasoning with them won't aggravate."

—Tongue Fu!'ism

Make People Feel Heard, Not Hassled

What do you do when someone comes to you feeling forlorn? Do you try to comfort him? Do you try to make him feel better?

Those intentions are meant to help, but they often backfire.

How so? When people are unhappy, they don't want advice or opinions, they want to be heard. Here's an example.

A teacher came home from school after a particularly frustrating day, threw her books and papers down on the dining room table and announced, "I quit!"

Her husband said in alarm, "You can't quit, we've got a mortgage to pay!"

She continued letting out her frustration, "Those kids don't appreciate everything I do for them. I pay for supplies out of my own pocket. I open my classroom early so they have a place to hang out. I stay late to help them with their homework. They don't notice and they don't care."

He countered with, "Sure they do. Remember last week Trudy came up, said you were her favorite teacher, and she wanted to grow up to be just like you?"

She kept letting off steam, "This is the unfriendliest school I've ever worked at. I've not made one friend since the beginning of the school year."

Trying to be helpful, he asked, "Well, have you extended yourself? You know, in order to have a friend, you have to be a friend."

Yikes. Could be another night on the couch for him.

What's interesting about this exchange is the husband was doing his best to help. He pointed out that her students *did* appreciate her. He suggested she reach out to others to make friends. In his mind, he was being supportive.

In her mind though, he wasn't being supportive, he was giving unsolicited advice. Instead of consoling her, he was contradicting her.

This urge to aid with advice, when all people want is to have a shoulder to cry on, is the source of countless misunderstandings. What could the husband have done instead? What can we do when someone comes to us unhappy?

Reflect, Don't Refute

"It is a luxury to be understood." —Ralph Waldo Emerson

Reflect what they're saying by paraphrasing it back. Notice, I didn't say parrot it back. Don't repeat it word for word, or else they'll look at you and say, "That's what I just said!" Put what they said in your own words so they know you understood.

When his wife threw her books down and said, "I quit," the husband could have said, "So, it was one of those kinds of days, huh?"

She would have probably given a heartfelt "Yeah!" and then continued with, "Those kids don't understand everything I do for them." He could have said, "So you go out of your way for the kids and they don't seem to appreciate it?"

She probably would have given another from-the-gut "Yeah!" and then continued with, "It's just the unfriendliest school I've ever worked at."

At this point, instead of intervening with *reasoning* and telling her what she should do, it would have been smarter to intervene with *wishes*, "I guess you wish this school was as friendly as Lakeland was, right?"

She probably would have agreed with another emphatic "Yes!"

Do you see what's happening? When we're trying to get something off our chest, and someone feeds back what we've been saying, we almost involuntarily say "Yeah!" because that person is vocalizing how we feel. As Emerson so eloquently stated, we are experiencing that luxurious feeling of being *understood*.

Being understood is so rare, yet it is what we want when we're feeling despondent. We don't want someone to tell us how we should feel, how we shouldn't feel, or what we should have done. We want someone to commiserate.

Have you ever had the blessed experience of pouring out your soul, and instead of the other person weighing in with their opinion, they simply let you get it off your chest? After purging your frustration, didn't you immediately feel better? It wasn't as if your situation was solved or that it had disappeared. It was just that there was another human being out there who knew how you felt. You were no longer alone with your misery. You had connected with someone who cared enough to let you get it off your chest, which got it out of your system.

Use the Therapist's Tool

> "You can't reason someone out of something they weren't reasoned into." —Jonathan Swift

This is what therapists do so well. They don't try to talk you *out* of your problems; they talk you *through* your problems. Imagine you went to a counselor to help you figure out whether to stay in teaching. Her first question is probably along the lines of, "So, tell me why you came here today."

You may say, "Well, I'm thirty-five years old, and I make $28,000 a year. All my friends who went to college make twice, even three times what I do. I have to work a second job just to pay my bills. I love teaching, but I don't know how much longer I can keep this up."

At that point, the therapist would probably ask, "So you're wondering if you should stay in this profession?"

Her paraphrasing confirms what you've just said and helps you continue to explore how you feel. You say, "You want to know how dedicated I am? I work nights at a Barnes & Noble so I can get a discount on the books I buy, out of my own pocket mind you, for my students. The thing is, I'll never be able to afford to buy a home on this salary. I don't want to live in an apartment for the rest of my life."

"So, you're conflicted because you love what you do, but it's not paying enough to support the lifestyle you want."

Notice, the therapist didn't chime in with her own opinion: "Please don't quit. We need teachers like you." She didn't join the rant: "I think it's terrible you get paid so little. That's outrageous." She didn't try to redirect her focus to something positive: "Maybe you don't get paid as much as you deserve, but it must be gratifying knowing you're making a difference."

She didn't pursue her own agenda, she helped you pursue yours. By mirroring what you're saying, instead of minimizing it, the therapist helps you release what's in you. This cathartic process is the purpose of paraphrasing.

The word "catharsis" means a "purgation that brings about spiritual renewal or release from tension," "elimination of a complex (fear or panic) by bringing it to consciousness and affording it expression." By restating what someone's saying (instead of refuting it) we help people identify and release what's bothering them, which is what they need. *After* they purge their angst, not before, they'll be ready to focus on what corrective action can be taken.

Are You Listening or Lecturing?

"We want people to feel with us more than to act for us."
—George Eliot

"I really needed to hear this," one teacher told me. "Eighteen of the twenty-three children in my class have parents who are either already divorced or in the process of a divorce. Several of my students are currently involved in nasty custody disputes, and half of them split time between their parents. It breaks my heart to see these kids put in the middle. Some of the stories they tell would curl your hair. It makes me want to hunt their parents down and read 'em the riot act. Don't they realize the damage they're doing to their kids?

"Yesterday Tiffany came to me in tears and told me her father was moving away and she wasn't going to see him anymore. She said between sobs, 'He doesn't love me anymore.' I was about to reassure her with, 'Honey, he does too love you,' when I realized she didn't need me disagreeing with her. Instead I asked, 'You're afraid he doesn't love you anymore because he's moving away?'

"She nodded and more tears came, 'He and my mom fight all the time.' Instead of offering some well-intended platitude like, 'Well, honey, sometimes adults fight. It doesn't mean they don't love you,' I said, 'So you wish they wouldn't fight so much?'

"She said, 'Yeah, it's my fault they broke up. They argue about me and my little brother all the time.' I wanted to tell her, 'It's not your fault they broke up,' but I realized she needed to voice her fears and feelings, not have them invalidated. I just kept paraphrasing what she said and coming in with wishes instead of reasoning. After a few minutes, she gave me a hug, wiped her face, and said, 'Thanks, Miss Jones,' and ran off to play.

"I want so much to 'fix' their problems, but I realize nothing I can say can make them go away. What I can do is make sure these kids know they have someone they can go to who will listen, who will be there for them."

Emotions Don't Respond to Logic

"No one wants advice—only corroboration." —John Steinbeck

This is such an important point. When we care about people, we don't want them to be unhappy. If they're hurting, our first instinct is to make things better for them. We want to come to their rescue and tell them what they ought to do to alleviate their suffering. However, when people are unhappy, they don't want someone telling them what they should do or how they should feel. What they want is for someone to listen. *That* is how we can make people feel better, not by trying to tell them their feelings are unfounded. People want their feelings to be acknowledged, not contested.

We naively think that if we tell people their fears are groundless, those fears will go away. The fact is, feelings are emotions, and emotions do not respond to logic. They are not erased simply because someone tells us they're not valid or true. We may think we're doing people a favor by telling that what they're feeling is wrong. Instead of doing them a favor, we're doing them a disservice. Not only do they feel bad, they've just been told they have no right to feel bad, so they feel worse.

What to do? Don't try to talk people *out* of their emotions, talk them *through* their emotions. Instead of refuting what they've said, feed back what they've said so they can thoroughly explore it and release it. Don't contest their point of view, corroborate it.

Please understand, once and for all, that people have a right to their feelings. Our role is not to try to get them to abandon what they're feeling; our role is to give them an opportunity to express what they're feeling. Then, and only then, will we have truly communicated, as defined by an "exchange of meaning."

Don't Say, "I Know Just How You Feel"

"No one ever listened himself out of a job." —Calvin Coolidge

Whatever you do, don't tell 'em, "I know just how you feel." They're likely to growl back, "You *don't* know how I feel."

Likewise, it may not help to let them know you've been in the same boat. If you say, "That happened to me one time," you may think it will alleviate their suffering to let them know you've gone through the same thing. In fact, it may shut them down because they think you're switching the focus to yourself. Telling them "We've all gone through this" may aggravate them even more because the underlying message is, "Quit your whining. This is no big deal. You're just one of many."

Unhappiness is a very individual thing. Later on, it might help the person to connect with others who have gone through the same experience. That's the purpose of support groups—to give us an opportunity to meet with kindred spirits so we can share common experiences. But for now, to be told, "Everyone gets hurt at one time or another. You'll get over it," will only invalidate their angst.

It's better to empathize with their angst rather than try to eliminate it. To modify Coolidge's observation, "No one ever listened himself out of a friend, either."

Tongue Fu! Tip for Teens

Your best friend didn't get accepted to the college of her choice. She's really bummed and you're trying to make her feel better. Unfortunately, no matter what you say, she continues to be in a funk. Remember, what she really wants right now is not well-meaning advice on how to get on with her life—she wants someone to listen.

Put yourself in her place and imagine how you would feel if you had your heart set on getting into a certain college, only to have your hopes dashed. When you imagine what it'd be like to have just received that rejection letter, you realize you wouldn't want someone trying to placate you with, "Guess it wasn't meant to be. Don't worry. You'll get into another college."

When you put yourself in your friend's place, you realize you'd want sympathy, not someone telling you to get over it. Give your friend what she wants, an empathetic ear: "You were really hoping to get into Tech, weren't you?"

She may wail, "I loved everything about it. I don't understand why I didn't get in. I've got a good GPA and my SATs were in the 1300s."

Resist the urge to come in with any type of "helpful" explanation, for example, "Well, I heard they had 18,000 applications for 4,000 spots. I just think they just had too many people to choose from. Maybe if you had applied for a different major. . . ."

Understand your friend doesn't really want a dialogue right now. She doesn't want to be convinced that she doesn't have a right to feel down. She wants to wallow in her disappointment for a bit. Simply say, "I'm sorry you didn't get in. I know you were really looking forward to it."

In awhile, she'll have worked through her setback by being able to express how she feels without being told she should feel differently, and she'll be ready to move on. And you will have been a good friend who helped her talk through her emotions instead of trying to talk her out of them.

Action Plan for Make People Feel Heard, Not Hassled

Your son just came home from school, upset because the soccer coach wants him to play goalie instead of forward. Your son has played forward since he first started playing soccer, and he loves scoring points. He's thinking of quitting the team because he's so unhappy about being assigned to this position. What do you do?

Words to Lose	Words to Use
You try to make him feel better and he feels hassled. *"I'm sure Coach has his reasons. You should be honored that he trusts you with that important job."*	You paraphrase back what he's saying and he feels heard. *"So, you're disappointed that you're not going to be able to play your same position?"*
You try to logically explain the circumstances so he won't feel so bad. *"Well, you know you can't always play the position you want when you're on a team."*	You acknowledge his emotions and let him know you understand why he feels so bad. *"I understand why you want to keep playing forward after all these years."*
You try to reason with him and he feels lectured to. *"Someone has to play goalie. You're the best player so it makes sense that he picked you."*	You intervene with wishes and he feels listened to. *"So you wish you could be in a position to score points like you've been doing?"*
You give unsolicited advice and let him know something similar happened to you. *"Look on the bright side. My coach did the same thing to me and I ended up being MVP."*	You empathize and let him work through his frustration rather than trying to talk him out of it. *"Have you talked to Coach about how you feel? Do you think that might help?"*

15

"Behind every argument lies someone's ignorance."

—Louis D. Brandeis

Don't Know What to Say? Say This

Would you like to know what to do when your mind goes blank?

First, it's important to know what NOT to do. If someone has made an unfair accusation, don't deny it.

If someone says, "You women are so emotional," and you protest with, "We are *not* emotional!" you've just unintentionally proven his or her point.

If someone says, "Why are you always on the defensive?" and you object with, "I'm not on the defensive!"—uh-oh, now you are!

From now on, if someone says something outrageous and your mind goes "duh," just say these four words, "What do you mean?"

Reveal the Real Issue Instead of Reacting to Accusations

"One half of the troubles in this world can be traced to saying 'yes' too soon and 'no' too late." —Josh Billings

With all due respect to Mr. Billings, I think half of the troubles in this world can be traced to us saying the first thing that comes to mind, regardless of whether it's going to help or hurt.

The purpose of this chapter is to point out that when we don't know what to say, it's often because the other person has said something so outrageous, we're tongue-tied. We are knocked back on our mental heels by this preposterous accusation that came out of nowhere. Though our first instinct is to angrily deny it, that will only serve to escalate the situation.

Instead of "biting the bait," simply put the conversational ball back in their court by asking, "What do you mean?" or "Why do you think that?" The beauty of these questions is they cause accusers to explain themselves, which often reveals what's really going on. Once we know what's at the root of their allegation, we can address that instead of simply reacting to their attack.

A woman who had recently been promoted to head up her department said, "I wish I'd known this last week. I was working in my office when one of our teachers, someone I've worked with for almost ten years, came in and said, 'You should never have been given this position. Face it, you weren't meant to be a manager.'

"Her criticism cut me to the quick. I said, 'Lois, I've been putting in sixty-hour weeks. I've been doing everything I can to improve conditions in this department.'

"She went on, 'It's not for lack of trying, I'll give you that. It's just that you're too nice to be a supervisor.'

"Then I said something I instantly regretted, 'Lois, are you sure this isn't sour grapes because you thought you should have gotten this promotion?' She marched out in a huff and we haven't spoken since.

"In retrospect, it would have been better if I had just asked, 'What do you mean?' Who knows, she could have been upset because a couple of our teachers have been coming in late and I haven't done anything about it. Maybe she didn't like the fact that we haven't had any staff meetings for several months and there's been some miscommunication. At least I would have understood *why* she criticized me instead of just jumping in with both feet and making things worse."

Answer Accusations with Questions

"Envy is almost always based on a complete misunderstanding of the other person's circumstances." —Tongue Fu'ism

A complete misunderstanding of the other person's circumstances can also cause anger. If we take a moment to go beyond what they've said and explore their rationale, we can often put an end to any tension. Reacting defensively to voiced dissatisfaction often aggravates more dissatisfaction. Requesting more information can instead help us uncover the source of their dissatisfaction, and from there we can take steps to eliminate it.

Want an example? A teacher walked into her classroom after a rainy weekend and discovered a puddle of water in the middle of the floor. She called the janitor and asked him to please come and mop it up.

The next day, after even more rain, the puddle was back in the middle of the floor. She called the janitor again and he came back and cleaned it up.

The rains kept coming and the puddle was even bigger the following day. This time, she didn't even call the janitor, she called the head custodian and asked him to please do something about the puddle. He showed up at her door a few minutes later and didn't even have a mop.

Flustered, she asked, "How are you going to mop up the puddle?"

With a twinkle in his eyes, the wise custodian replied, "I'm not. I'm going to fix the leak."

When people make a unfair accusation, we often take umbrage and either defend ourselves or deny their charge, the verbal equivalents of mopping up the puddle but leaving the cause of the mess.

Asking "What do you mean?", "What makes you think that?", or "Why do you say that?" goes to the source of their "leak," and we can fix that instead of battling back and forth about whether their claim is true or untrue.

Use Tact Instead of Attacking Back

"Tact is, after all, a kind of mind-reading." —Sarah Orne Jewett

"Tact" (defined as "sensitive perception, skill, and grace in dealing with people, a keen sense of what to do or say in order to avoid offense and maintain good relations with others") is a commitment to look beyond the obvious and unearth the motive. When we do that, we can often "heal" what's wrong at its root.

So, what are you going to do next time someone says something that hurts your feelings? Are you going to deny or defend their accusation? Could you instead look beyond their surface behavior to its source? Could you do some mind-reading to intuit what's really going on? Asking questions instead of firing back a retort that's on the tip of your tongue can help you uncover the basis for their behavior. You can then address the underlying cause, rather than merely attacking back.

Tongue Fu! Tip for Teens

Do you have a quick temper? If you are quick to take offense, it's in your best interests to learn to ask before you react. Instead of assuming you know what people mean, ask them what they mean. You may be surprised how often people say things that "just came out wrong." They didn't intend to be cruel or unkind, they just spoke without thinking—which is good reason for you to get more information before you fire back.

A friend was driving a group of teens to a football game. One of them, Chris, had just been elected by the junior class to be their junior–senior prom prince. The guys were razzing him about it, and he was taking it good-naturedly until one of them said half-seriously, "I think Scott should have got it."

My friend could tell Chris was kind of hurt by his friend's remark, but he didn't say anything, and the conversation moved on.

Later on, at the game, she asked her son's friend why he thought Scott should have been the prince. He explained, "Chris has been class king every single year since junior high. Scott's mom has cancer and is in the hospital, and I think it'd mean a lot more to him to be prince."

She could tell he hadn't meant any harm, so she asked, "How do you think Chris felt when you said that?" He shrugged it off initially and said, "He knows I'm just kidding."

She said, "I'm not sure he did. He looked a little hurt by it." The teen said, "I'll clear it up with him. I didn't mean it that way."

Exactly. We have reasons for saying the things we do. But if the people hearing them don't know our reasons, or if they misunderstand our reasons, they end up with hurt feelings, and we could end up with a broken friendship.

A lot of this can be avoided. Next time someone says something you don't like, don't take offense. Ask, "What you do mean by that?" Doing so could turn a potential argument into an understanding and both of you will be better off.

Action Plan for Don't Know What To Say? Say This

You have an IEP meeting with a parent to discuss the special needs of her daughter. The daughter has a learning disability and has a private aide assigned to help her take notes and read. The mother is known as a tireless advocate for her child. No sooner do you sit down for your appointment when the mother starts with, "You don't care about my daughter." How do you respond?

Words to Lose	Words to Use
You give an emotional denial which sets up a "Yes I do, No you don't" argument. *"That's not true. I do everything I can to help Crystal."*	You ask, "What do you mean?" to find out what's behind her accusation. *"What makes you feel that way?"*
You don't know what to say so you say the first thing that comes to mind. *"I've been teaching for ten years, and no one's ever complained before."*	You take the time to ask a question instead of blurting out what's on the tip of your tongue. *"Why do you feel Crystal isn't getting the attention she needs?"*
You take offense at her unfair allegation. *"I spend all the time I can with her, considering I have twenty other students to take care of."*	You try to get to the root of her allegation. *"So, you feel she's falling behind and she doesn't know how to complete her assignments?"*
You make the situation worse by focusing on a hurtful statement. *"You don't seem to understand how hard it is to give everyone individual attention in such a large class."*	You "fix the leak" by resolving the root of the problem. *"Can we set up an appointment with Crystal, you, her aide, and myself to see what we can do?"*

16

"Part of the happiness of life consists not in fighting battles but in avoiding them.

A masterly retreat is in itself a victory."

—Norman Vincent Peale

Graciously Exit No-Win Disputes

Have you ever been in a heated discussion where you could tell you're not going to change the other person's mind, and they're not going to change yours?

Would you like to know what to do next time you're at loggerheads and you're afraid you're both about to say something you'll regret?

Sidestep that stalemate by saying, "You know what, we're both right," and then move on to a less contentious topic.

I can imagine you're thinking, "What?!"

Remember, in many disputes it's not that one side is totally right and one side is totally wrong. You may have radically different opinions; however, that's what they are—*opinions*. Each of you probably has valid reasons for thinking the way you do. The two of you may not agree, but that shouldn't make you mortal enemies. You simply have different points of view.

Turn Reproach into Reconciliation

"The overall purpose of human communication is—or should be—reconciliation." —M. Scott Peck

Part of Tongue Fu! is realizing, in the heat of the moment, that no matter how strongly we feel about an issue, the person we're dealing with feels just as strongly that their view is true. We could argue for hours and not alter each other's thinking. Why battle back and forth saying hurtful things when it's not going to accomplish anything of value?

Hopefully, one of you will have the presence of mind in the midst of a knock-down, drag-out argument to admit that *both* of you have valid reasons to think the way you do, and it's in both of your best interests to move the discussion to a topic that's not nearly as volatile or relationship-destroying.

At a recent state education conference, a break-out session was scheduled to discuss the implementation and ramifications of the "No Child Left Behind" policy. Within minutes, the participants were angrily debating the relative merits of the program. Some felt it was idealistic and logistically impossible to carry out. Others felt it was a visionary policy that deserved praise. Three panelists started arguing amongst themselves, and audience members were shouting for the floor and trying to commandeer the aisle microphone.

The program moderator was finally able to get the chaos under control and reconcile the discordant group by saying, "First, let's recognize this is a controversial issue and we all have strong opinions about it. Let's also recognize that opinions are just that, opinions. No one is right or wrong here. We all care about the education of our children. We may have different ideas about how to carry out that education; however, *we are on the same side*. Let's agree to treat each other with respect." He then went on to establish ground rules for the remainder of the session so panelists and participants had an opportunity to contribute their opinions in an orderly way. (We'll talk about those ground rules in chapter 20, "Lay Down the Laws.")

Disengage from Disagreements with Dignity

"To think is to differ." —Clarence Darrow

Notice the wonderful phrase the moderator used, "*We're on the same side.*" This is such a helpful thing to say in the middle of a verbal clash because it reminds us that while we may have different approaches, we often have the same goal.

Imagine you and your spouse disagree about how to discipline your teenager. He has been coming home past curfew, and several times you've caught him in a lie, saying he was at a friend's house when he wasn't. You feel your partner is too punitive and your partner thinks you're too permissive. Your discussion about how to deal with your son turns into a family feud.

Your partner says, "He's never going to respect us if we don't start showing him who's boss." You say, "He's just going to become more rebellious if we ground him." Your spouse comes back with, "It's our house and our rules. If he wants to live here, he's going to have to abide by them." You point out, "He's going to be eighteen in a few months, legally an adult. We can't treat him like he's a child." And so on.

Mentally step back for a moment and look at where this is going. Neither of you are making any headway. You're only going to become more and more upset with each other, which isn't going to serve your marriage or the situation with your son. Before you become a house divided against itself, use these relationship-saving words, "*Hey, we want the same thing.*" That one sentence can remind you that you're not opponents, that you have the same objective—to raise a healthy, well-adjusted, well-behaved son. That perspective-restoring phrase can help you stop seeing each other as the problem and guide you back into working together as a team to resolve a shared concern.

Help Both Parties Save Face

"We may not always see eye to eye. We can try to see heart to heart." —Sam Levenson

The point of this chapter is to provide phrases that can help us diplomatically disengage from a disagreement when it's apparent we're about to come to verbal blows. The challenge is, people with strong opinions are often attached to their positions and will likely be reluctant to reverse themselves. They may dig in their mental heels and persist in resisting. That's why we need to give people a way to back away without having to back down.

The following phrases can give antagonists a face-saving out that doesn't make them wrong and doesn't force them to reverse themselves.

- "Let's agree to disagree on this one."
- "You know what, we're both right."
- "Hey, it's important for us to remember we're on the same side."
- "Different strokes for different folks."
- "It's six of one, a half dozen of another."
- "Just because we don't see eye to eye doesn't mean we have to be enemies."
- "We want the same thing. We may have different ways of getting there, but we have the same destination."
- "We could argue 'til the cows come home, and we're never going to agree. Let's talk about something else."
- "We have diametrically opposed opinions on this, and we're not going to change each other's mind. Let's make this a hands-off topic and call a truce."
- "You say tomato, I say tomato. To each his own."
- "This serves no good purpose. The more we talk about this, the more upset we're both going to get. Let's drop it and move on."
- "This is a no-win. Next subject."

Identify Your "Hands-Off" Topics

"Include me out." —Samuel Goldwyn

What are your "hands-off" topics? Perhaps you and your teacher's aide disagree about politics. Maybe you and a fellow counselor disagree about mainstreaming. Perhaps you and your principal have opposing views about academic/athletic eligibility rules. Maybe two peers are gossiping and you don't want any part of it.

Before getting into it with another person, ask yourself, "Is there any chance of a positive outcome to this discussion?" If so, by all means, proceed. If you know in advance, however, that broaching this topic will serve no good purpose, save yourself a lot of pointless frustration by putting both hands up in an "I surrender" posture and repeating Goldwyn's bon mot, "Include me out."

A teachers' union rep once asked me, "What if we're in a negotiation and we've reached an impasse? We don't want to walk away from the table; however, the administrators aren't willing to budge and neither are we."

When you sense you're both locked into a position and neither side is going to "blink," give everyone a face-saving out by taking that particular issue off the table for now. Say, "Let's come back to this one," and switch attention to a portion of the contract negotiation that's not so volatile. That phrase allows you to change the focus of the discussion without having to change your mind.

By concentrating on a section of the contract that's less controversial, you can reestablish a more amicable atmosphere. After a spirit of collaboration has been restored, you can return to that original stumbling block and tackle it when everyone's more predisposed to work together cooperatively.

So, what are you going to do next time you're engaged in, or about to engage in, a no-win debate? Use one of these face-saving phrases to detour around the dispute and move on to a more mutually beneficial interaction.

Tongue Fu! Tip for Teens

Let me save you a lot of grief right now. There are times friends will ask for your opinion. And they're not really looking for honest feedback, they're looking for reinforcement. The classic, "Do you think these jeans make me look fat?" comes to mind. Understand there is no "right" answer to that question. If you say yes, the next thing you know your friend will be upset because you think she's fat (even though you didn't say that). If you say no, she'll accuse you of not telling the truth. See? No win.

It's better just to stay out of these situations altogether. How do you do that? Back away, shaking your head in mock horror, saying, "No way am I going to answer that. Anything I say could be taken the wrong way."

If two classmates are putting down a third and they ask, "What do you think of him?," remember you can refuse to "play." Say, "Leave me out of this one." Don't allow people to pressure you into saying something you'd rather not. And don't allow yourself to put your mouth in motion before you put your brain in gear. Taking a moment to think before you spout is a lot easier than trying to put words back in your mouth after they've been let out.

Action Plan for Graciously Exit No-Win Disputes

You stop by the teachers' lounge to get a cup of coffee and walk into the middle of a gripe session. Several peers are bemoaning the quality of substitute teachers. One says, "Face it, we're so desperate, we're settling for warm bodies." One turns to you and asks, "What do you think?" What do you say?

Words to Lose	Words to Use
You get drawn into a pointless debate. *"Uhhmm. Well, I know the woman they have teaching math doesn't even understand calculus."*	You avoid a pointless debate. *"All I want is a cup of coffee. Just pretend I'm not here."*
You contribute your point of view, which just perpetuates the grumbling. *"And I've heard the history teacher is three pages ahead of her students."*	You choose not to contribute to the grumbling. *"Thanks, but no thanks. Leave me out of this."*
You continue to share your opinions about this no-win topic. *"Can you believe they get paid almost as much as we do, and we have M.Ed.'s?"*	You try to move the conversation off this no-win topic. *"No matter what we say, it's not going to change things. Let's talk about Teacher Institute Day."*
People are inflexible and continue to see only their own point of view. *"We should file a protest. These subs are glorified baby-sitters. They shouldn't be teaching."*	You get creative and come with a face-saving out. *"Let's agree to disagree about this. Come on, we only have ten minutes before class. Who's going to the program on Saturday?"*

17

"He knew the precise psychological moment to say nothing."

—Oscar Wilde

Use Tongue Glue!

Previous chapters have pointed out how we can focus on solutions, ask "What do you mean?," and graciously exit no-win disputes.

Would you like to know one of the best ways to prevent conflicts altogether? Don't say anything at all. That's called Tongue Glue!

Silence Can Be the Ultimate Diplomacy

"It is better to swallow words than to have to eat them later."
—Franklin D. Roosevelt

It can be hard to hold your tongue when you've been wronged. You may be sorely tempted to tell that person exactly what you think of him or her. As Roosevelt pointed out though, if you give in to that urge, you may be eating those words (along with a little crow) later.

A seminar participant burst out laughing when I shared the Roosevelt quote with our group. He said, "I learned that the hard way on a blind date. In the first few awkward moments of exchanging our life histories, I discovered my date used to live in my hometown. She asked if I had known Mrs. Walford. Without really thinking about it, I said, 'That old hag? She was my high school English teacher.'

"I went on to explain that I had hated her class and she had flunked me. I noticed too late that my date had an odd expression on her face. When I finally wound down, she said in a rather strangled voice, 'Mrs. Walford is my stepmother.' Arggh! The evening went downhill from there and couldn't get over soon enough for either of us."

If only that young man had practiced Tongue Glue!. Tongue Glue! is simply asking ourselves, "Could what I'm about to say come back to haunt me?" If it's likely we could regret what we're about to say, it shouldn't be said.

Bite that Tongue

"I never regretted a single thing I didn't say." —Calvin Coolidge

Imagine you're interviewing for a teaching position at a different school in your district. The interview is going well until the final question when the principal asks why you're leaving your current job. The reason you're looking for work elsewhere is because you don't get along with your current principal.

Please understand bad-mouthing your boss will only reflect negatively on you. Even if the interviewer knows your principal and agrees with your less-than-positive opinion, she'll think less of you for being indiscrete. She may even worry that someday you'd make similar disparaging remarks about her. As a message on a church bulletin board once put it, "Anyone who gossips *to* us will gossip *about* us."

Refuse to give in to the urge to (as they say in Hawaii) "talk stink." No matter how justified your comments, no one will respect you for trashing your supervisor, least of all a potential new employer. Simply say, "I've heard wonderful things about what you're accomplishing here at your school, and I'm excited about the possibility of joining your staff." If, for some reason, you're pressed about your feelings about your current principal, simply say, "I learned a lot from him [or her]." That neutral statement is undoubtedly true and is a diplomatic way to answer the question without airing the dirty laundry.

Silence Can Be More Powerful than Words

> "The real art of conversation is not only to say the right thing
> in the right place, but to leave unsaid the wrong thing at the
> tempting moment." —Dorothy Nevill

Tongue Glue! is not only a tool for keeping us from blurting out something we can't take back, it is also a tool for motivating people to see a point of view other than their own.

Do you remember the suggestion that we ask ourselves, "How would I feel?" to see things from other people's perspective? You may have been thinking, "I try to do that. What if someone isn't seeing *my* side of the situation?"

Here's what you can do next time someone is stubbornly refusing to listen to you. Verbally paint the situation, then ask, "What do you suggest?" and *stop talking*. Don't say anything else. Just let the silence sit. That question, coupled with the quiet, subtly forces the other person to put themselves in your shoes. Because you're not bombarding them with words, they're not resisting your verbiage.

That question causes them to put themselves in the role of problem solver. Instead of standing there with their mental arms crossed, they're experiencing things from your point of view. They will often come up with a viable solution when moments before they weren't even open to ideas.

Years ago, I was asked by the University of California at Los Angeles to present a workshop on ConZentration. I arrived at the hotel the evening before the talk and asked for the box of handouts that had been shipped ahead. The staff, after much searching, couldn't find it. These handouts were an important part of the program. I didn't have an original or a disk with me (my bad), so my only option was to re-create and duplicate the material that night.

You'll know this was l-o-n-g ago, because it was before twenty-four-hour copy centers like Kinko's existed. I was stymied until I spied a computer in the hotel office. I explained my situation to the front desk manager and asked if I could use their equipment if I promised to take good care of it and pay for supplies.

He turned me down flat. You can probably guess his rationale for refusing my request, "If we let *you* use our computer, we'd have to let *everybody* use our computer."

I understood his reluctance. He didn't know if he could trust me, and it was an unusual request. It was a lot easier to say no than it was to say yes. I knew, though, that I would use their equipment responsibly and this could be a win-win if I gently persisted. So I explained the situation without raising my voice: "These handouts were shipped more than two weeks ago. When I called yesterday to confirm they'd arrived, a staff member said they had. Now they can't be found, and fifty-five executives from this area will be attending this program tomorrow in your conference center and expecting this support material. What do you suggest?"

I then zipped my lip.

The employee hemmed and hawed. I bit my tongue to keep from rescuing him. My continued silence compelled him to "own" the problem and feel some obligation for resolving it instead of brushing me off with a perfunctory "No way." Finally he relented, "All right, you can use our computer and copier. Just be careful!" I did and I was.

I also took the time to write a letter to the general manager expressing my appreciation for the employee's above and beyond assistance in my time of need.

Silence Can Be Our Most Persuasive Form of Communication

"There is much to be said for not saying much." —Frank Tyger

I am not suggesting we use silence as a power play to manipulate people into giving us what we want. I am suggesting that silence, coupled with "What do you suggest?" can break through someone's stubborn refusal to consider viable options. If I had obnoxiously directed my anger at the hotel employee, he would have had no incentive to help me. By calmly describing the situation, asking for his recommendation, and quietly waiting while he thought things through, I gave him the mental space and motivation to come up with a workable solution.

Next time your temper's about to get the best of you and an unhelpful retort is on the tip of your tongue, what are you going to do? As a popular T-shirt in Vermont says, "Don't talk unless you can improve the silence." Good policy.

Tongue Fu! Tip for Teens

I feel blessed because my teenaged sons occasionally help me with my presentations, and we get to travel to fun speaking locations. They've sold books and tapes in the back of the room on cruise ships, in Las Vegas, and in resort hotels on Maui. As a result, they've listened to many Tongue Fu! programs and can often supply the punch lines to my stories.

I asked which of these ideas they've found most helpful, and Tom (now studying physics and astronomy at Virginia Tech) said, "It's the idea about not bad-mouthing others 'cause it can come back to bite us, and it never accomplishes anything positive. Smart young man, that Tom. (Of course, I'm partial.)

Part of adolescence consists of learning to control the urges bombarding our senses so we can conduct ourselves in responsible ways. Instead of saying what we want, when we want, we learn socially appropriate ways to act and interact. It helps to have personal guidelines that keep us from blurting out things that could cause irreversible damage. I think one of the easiest of these is to simply adopt a policy that says, "If I'm hot under the collar and about to let someone know exactly what I think of them, I'm going to stop and ask myself, 'Will this help or will it hurt?' If it won't help, and it could hurt, I'm going to hold my tongue instead of let loose."

Action Plan for Use Tongue Glue!

The PTA vice president opens the monthly meeting by announcing that the president has resigned and she is now in charge. Afterwards, you encounter several parents discussing a rumor they've heard through the grapevine that the president has been involved in some questionable business practices and is about to be indicted. They ask if you've heard anything. What do you do?

Words to Lose	Words to Use
You speak up before stopping to think whether it could backfire. *"Shady real estate dealings? I wondered how he could afford that fancy house."*	You think first so you don't say something you regret. *You are silent for a moment while you ask yourself, "Would saying something hurt or help?"*

Words to Lose	Words to Use
You join in on the gossip and add to the hearsay. *"A friend of mind who's a district attorney said they're going to be bringing charges by the end of the week."*	You act with integrity and choose not to bad-mouth. *"I don't have anything to say about this."*
You say what's on the tip of your tongue. *"I never trusted the guy. He always seemed kind of smarmy to me."*	You practice Tongue Glue! *"I thought Carol did a good job handling the meeting, didn't you?"*

18

"He who never changes his opinions and never corrects his mistakes, will never be wiser on the morrow than he is today."

—Tyrone Edwards

Approach with an Open Mind

Do you have an unpleasant history with someone, and the very sight of the person is enough to make you want to head the other direction? You know what that's called? Run Fu!

If you deal with a disagreeable person at school, and the very mention of his or her name is enough to make your teeth clench, this chapter's for you.

This is one of the most challenging aspects of dealing with people. When we've had multiple negative encounters with an individual, it's not easy to put our feelings aside and give them a clean slate. It's not easy; however, it's *necessary* if we have any hope of a constructive interaction.

At the Academy Awards one year, Sir Laurence Olivier was given an honorary award and delivered an eloquent acceptance speech. At least, people thought it was eloquent. The camera panned the audience and showed people with tears in their eyes, they were so moved by his remarks.

Backstage, actor Jon Voight complimented Olivier on his speech. Oliver demurred and said his talk wasn't that special; he had forgotten what he wanted to say. A disbelieving Voight argued that his presentation had been brilliant. Only when Voight watched the replay of the acceptance talk on the video monitor did he see for himself that it had been less than perfect.

How could this have happened? If Voight and the audience had *really* been listening, they would have been scratching their heads trying to make sense of Olivier's remarks. However, they hadn't been listening. They had prejudged Olivier based on his reputation as a marvelous orator and weren't concentrating on his words.

Are you wondering, "What's the point?" The point is, when we prejudge people based on their reputation, *positive or negative*, we don't really concentrate on the content of what they are saying. And that means we could be headed for a time-consuming, relationship-damaging misunderstanding.

Give 'Em a Chance

"A closed mind is a dying mind." —Edna Ferber

From now on, vow to approach people with an open mind rather than a made-up mind. How do you do that? When you run into people who have a bad "rep" and your judgment starts kicking in, say to yourself, "Give 'em a chance."

Tell yourself, "I don't know what they're going to say until *after* they say it, not when I see them coming down the hall."

A vice principal told me, "This is easier said than done. A lot of my job is handling disciplinary problems. I see the same kids in my office, week after week. How am I not supposed to see them as slackers when they're repeat offenders?"

I was glad he brought this up because it goes right to the heart of this issue. It's tempting to "label" kids when they've repeatedly caused problems. Unfortunately, as soon as we brand kids as troublemakers, we lock into that perception, which means we treat them like troublemakers— and if we treat them like troublemakers, they'll respond like troublemakers. We contribute to the unhealthy cycle by reinforcing and perpetuating the perception that they're good for nothing.

Imagine one of these "troublemakers" comes into your office. If you internally roll your eyes and greet him by saying, "Jerome, you again?! What is it this time?" you have just let this young man know he's already been found guilty even though he hasn't yet opened his mouth. How do you think that makes him feel? It probably fills him with resentment, which means he may mouth off. This fits right in with your view of him, and the scenario plays out . . . exactly as you thought it would.

Imagine instead that when he walks in, you remind yourself to "Give him a chance. I am going to listen as if this were the first time I met him." Who knows? Jerome might surprise you. He may respond to your respectful treatment by treating you with respect. Once you hear his side of the story (and you really *hear* it because you're listening instead of thinking "Here we go again"), you can determine what to do based on *this* incident rather than based on cumulative distaste for his previous behavior.

Please note, I'm not saying we shouldn't take into account someone's past behavior. However, we take their history into account *after* we've given them a chance and heard the facts about the situation.

Give People the Benefit of the Doubt

"Every year I grow more convinced it is wisest and best to fix our attention on the beautiful and good and dwell as little as possible on the evil and false." —Cecil

My walking buddy Karen told me, "It's not something we talk about very much, but many teachers will tell you there are 'good' years and 'not-so-good' years. Each class has its own personality and group dynamic.

"One eighth-grade class stands out in my mind as being unruly and unmotivated. The girls, who could usually be relied upon to be cooperative, were all in love with the toughest boy, and were no help at all.

"One day, Bubba remained in the room after the others had left. He was bigger than the others by at least a head, with broad shoulders. I was desperate and at my wit's end, so I decided to give him the benefit of the doubt and appeal to his better nature. I told him I needed his help controlling the class because, as things stood, we were going to end up accomplishing very little.

"My appeal seemed to enlist his sympathy. Who knows? Maybe no one had ever given him a chance to be a 'good guy' before. After our conversation, things changed dramatically. If the other students were rude to me, Bubba would intervene. If they got too loud, he would tell them to quiet down. I started asking Bubba to run errands, to secure AV equipment, etc. He seemed to feel good about having opportunities to be helpful. In fact, other teachers started to see special managerial talents in Bubba. He soon took over maintenance of all the AV equipment in the school. It gave me great pleasure to see him flying around the halls with a projector cart, trailed by other members of 'his' AV team. I hear he went on to run the entire AV department in high school. I never dreamed that giving Bubba a chance would make such a difference for me and for him. That is one of the miracles of teaching. Choosing to give them the benefit of the doubt can lead to something good that changes all parties for the better."

Let Go of Those Labels

"What is prejudice? An opinion, which is not based upon reason; a judgment, without having heard the facts."
—Carrie Chapman Catt

Prejudices can be particularly odious because they cause us to see people through the lens of our assumptions. We don't really "see" particular individuals. We draw conclusions and discriminate based on ethnic background, family history, economic status—whatever was drummed into us growing up.

Karl Menninger said, "Fears are educated into us, and can, if we wish, be educated out of us." *Prejudices* were also educated into us during our childhood by the significant adults in our life, and can, if we wish, be educated out of us.

The way to do this is to commit to drawing conclusions about someone based purely on our interactions with *that individual*—not on what we've heard about him or her (hearsay is faulty). Instead of making sweeping assumptions about "types" of people, we choose to believe everyone has the right to be judged on his or her individual behavior, not by his or her "category."

One young man, who happens to be African American, told me he still remembers the shock on the face of a schoolmate's mother when he showed up at their house on a weeknight to work on a group project. "I'm on the football team with her son. I have a 3.8 GPA, I'm on the student council, and I volunteer at our local food bank," but you'd never know it from the look on her face. She looked at me suspiciously, held the door half-closed, and said with a frown, "Can I help you?"

"I told her, 'I'm here to study with Kurt.' Instead of asking me in, she hesitated for a moment and said, 'could you wait here a minute?' then went downstairs to check if I was the right guy. I try not to be sensitive about stuff like that, but she probably would have welcomed me with open arms if I'd been white. The whole time I was there, she kept an eye on me, like I was going to steal their silver or something. The same thing happens when I go into stores. Security personnel follow me around like I'm a crime waiting to happen. It's not like I did anything to deserve this. I just happen to be one of the only black people in our town, and I pay for it every day of my life."

This young man deserves to be treated with courtesy, not suspicion. From now on, when you meet people for the first time or the fiftieth time, could you "give 'em a chance?" Could you promise yourself you'll only arrive at conclusions *after* you've heard what they have to say? Could you put assumptions aside and see people as the individuals they are, instead of a member of a category?

Pope John Paul II said, "The worst prison would be a closed heart." Choosing to approach people with an open mind and heart frees us to connect with people based on their character rather than on their color.

Tongue Fu! Tip for Teens

Part of being a teenager is living in the land of "cool" and "uncool." Yet, who decides that? Who decides kids in choir are uncool? Who decides if cheerleaders and quarterbacks are "in"? Who decides whether kids in ROTC or chess or shop are "out"?

The faceless mob, that's who. Could you elect not to buy into what others think? Could you decide to come to your own conclusions about who you like and don't like, who you trust and don't trust, and what group you want to be part of—based on *your* communications with those individuals, not on some nebulous stereotype that may have been passed down through the ages?

A young woman told me, "I moved from a farm community to a big college town to attend our state university. When my dorm roommate discovered I was from the 'boondocks'—her term—she took me under her wing. I'd played clarinet in high school and was looking forward to trying out for the marching band, but she told me they were a bunch of losers and warned me not to have anything to do with them.

"I was naive, and she was older and had grown up in that area, so I (incorrectly) thought she knew better than I did. I hung out with her that first semester and was miserable. She and her clique constantly took potshots at other people. It took me awhile to realize their put-downs said a lot more about them than they did about the people they were accusing of being nerds.

"I finally got fed up with her narrow-minded attitude and went my own way. I joined the band after semester break and ended up traveling all over the country with them to compete in parades and perform half-time shows. The first chair clarinetist, who was one of the 'losers' my roommate had warned me about became my best friend, and we still keep in touch. I can't believe I bought into her bigoted beliefs. It taught me a valuable lesson, though. I make up my own mind about people, instead of letting someone else make it up for me."

Could you learn from her example? Could you decide who you want to hang with based on *your* experience with them, instead of letting other people do your thinking for you? Have the courage to have a "mind of your own," and make sure it's open.

Action Plan for Approach with an Open Mind

You're in charge of your school's science fair. A parent e-mailed and volunteered to be a judge. You took one look at his very impressive qual-ifications and sent back an immediate confirmation. Your vice-chair finds out you've done this and is horrified. "Tell me you didn't do this. He's an arrogant know-it-all who has to prove to everyone how smart he is. E-mail him back and tell him the panel of judges has already been selected." What do you do?

Words to Lose	Words to Use
You adopt someone else's opinion of this person, sight unseen. *"Oh no, I can't believe I did this. He's going to make us all miserable."*	You decide to draw your own conclusions. *"Hey, let's give him a chance."*
You judge him solely by his reputation. *"I wish I'd known this before. I never would have said he could be a judge."*	You choose to withhold judgment until after you meet this person. *"Let's meet with him before we make any decisions."*
You make a sweeping generalization based on this person's "type." *"He's a military officer. No wonder he likes to boss people around."*	You elect to judge him on his performance, not his category. *"He's been a physicist for years. Let's keep an open mind*
You fit everything he says and does into your preconceptions and prejudices. *"See, there he goes, trying to show off. I should have listened to Brian."*	You keep an open mind and evaluate his behavior based on its merits. *"First, let's establish some groundrules about the judging so everyone has a chance to contribute."*

PART III

Take Responsibility for Resolving Conflicts

"The only thing necessary for the triumph of evil is for good men to do nothing."

—EDMUND BURKE

19

"Whether or not we support a decision depends a lot on whether it's being done to us, or by us."

—Tongue Fu'ism

Don't Take Control, Share Control

You may have noticed a trend that many conflicts are based on a battle for control. Someone is telling us we can't have or do something we want, and we don't like it. We're upset about the detrimental impact someone's having on our life and we "fight back" in an effort to regain control of our circumstances.

That's where Tongue Fu! comes in. The premise of Tongue Fu! is that by choosing to communicate in diplomatic ways, we can be a verbal "bridge over troubled waters." Even when circumstances aren't to our liking, we can communicate those circumstances in such a way that people will understand them. They may not like them; however, they'll understand them. What that means is that even when circumstances are less than satisfactory, we can continue to get along with each other instead of seeing each other as mortal enemies.

A doctor may not be able to miraculously cure a terminal patient, but she can choose to comfort the patient with caring communication. Her sensitive words may not be able to improve the sad circumstances, but they can soften them.

Sometimes our communication *can* improve the circumstances. If conflict is usually based on a battle for control, then it makes sense that if we could find a way to give both parties involved more control, they would no longer have any need to battle each other. Right? We can eliminate or minimize the conflict by making control a nonissue.

From now on, if you and another person are at loggerheads, ask yourself, "Is this a battle for control?" If it is (and it probably is), ask yourself if there's a way you can *share* control, instead of one person being *in* control and the other person feeling *out of* control. Want to know how and why this works? Read on.

Pose Options and Let Them Decide

"People are usually more convinced by reasons they discover themselves than by those found by others." —Blaise Pascal

A wise taxi driver was the first to introduce me to this concept. I was late wrapping up a workshop and only had an hour to catch my plane. I hailed a cab and quickly explained my plight. The cabby had obviously been around the block a few times and knew better than to set himself up for failure. He turned to me and asked respectfully, "We can take the freeway or the beach road. Which do you prefer?"

I deferred to him. "Whichever is fastest, please." He shook his head and said, "You choose." I picked the freeway and off we went. I wondered why he politely insisted on me making the decision and asked him about it.

He explained, "I've learned that when people are in a hurry, it's a mistake for me to select the route. If we get tied up in traffic and get delayed, guess who gets blamed? If the passenger chooses the route, and for some reason we don't make it on time, then *they* take responsibility instead of making it my fault."

Smart man. From now on, if you're facing a tough decision involving others, don't think things through on your own, arrive at the action to be taken, and then present it to the group as a fait accompli. If you do, even if it's the best option, the people affected will probably resist the plan and resent you. Why? The solution was presented *to* them instead of being processed *by* them.

A better approach is to develop two equally acceptable alternatives, pose them to the group, and ask them which they prefer. They'll be a lot happier with the decision because they made it.

Involve People in the Process

"It's coexistence or no existence." —Bertrand Russell

Notice I didn't suggest you turn the issue over to the group and give them carte blanche permission to produce a solution. As you're probably well aware, decision by committee is not always the most expeditious way to resolve an issue. Plus, when you turn a problem over to a group and ask them to come up with a plan, you've just given away the power. Now the group is in control. What if they come back with a solution that is not viable? Then you've set up double jeopardy. You've asked for their opinion, and you can't act on it. Ouch. It's better to pose options you know in advance are feasible. That way, you're keeping some control while giving some control. That's the definition of a win–win situation.

A government employee said "Yea, verily" to the above caveat. "A few years ago, our agency installed 'quality circles.' This idea works great in theory, but boy, did it backfire in reality. Management asked for volunteers from the different divisions and told us we would be meeting every other week to discuss how we could improve efficiency. In the entire time I was involved, they only instituted three of the suggestions we made. Sometimes we never even knew why they didn't follow up on our ideas. We started dropping out in droves when it became clear that our good intentions and hard work weren't going to be honored."

Please keep this man's experience in mind when you involve people in problem solving. Let participants know the parameters of their authority and set up a feedback loop so they're kept informed of the outcome of their recommendations.

An excellent example of how this can be done "right" was demonstrated by a local high school which had outgrown its gymnasium for graduation. This heated issue was debated in the local newspapers with alumni, parents, and faculty all arguing about the appropriate venue. Finally, the principal researched three options, put them on a ballot, and put it to a vote. The graduation could be held on the football field (for free), in an auditorium at a local junior college (for a small usage fee to be absorbed by the high school), or at a local hotel ballroom (graduates would get four free tickets and additional tickets would be $10 each). Each senior had two votes (one representing his/her preference and one representing the parents' preference). The votes were counted up and the majority ruled. Issue solved. Was everyone happy? No. However, *most* of the people were happy because the decision was made in a fair, timely way instead of the principal making a unilateral decision that alienated half his constituency.

Defer by Asking, "Which Do You Prefer?"

"Deference is silent flattery." —Josh Billings

Unilateral is defined as "done or undertaken by one person or party." It is also defined as "one-sided." No wonder people resent unilateral decisions. It means we are left out of the loop. It means someone made a decision on our behalf without consulting us.

There are certainly times in the school arena when it is appropriate to be an autocrat and make unilateral decisions. For example, attendance isn't an option. Taking a test isn't open to a vote. Conducting class isn't a democracy. Educators understand it's important to let students know who's in charge—and it's not the students.

However, there are many occasions throughout the day when we can pose options and let people choose, so they feel some type of inclusion and autonomy. This process of sharing control can be the social lubricant that helps us coexist cooperatively.

If a student asks a counselor, "Can I stop by this afternoon to talk with you about my SATs?" Instead of, "You'll have to make it tomorrow. I'm going to be in a meeting all afternoon," perhaps we could say, "Sure. I've got time during lunch or after school tomorrow. Which do you prefer?"

If someone asks, "Can someone help me with this new laptop? I don't know how to download attachments," instead of saying, "You'll have to talk to Tech Support. They handle that," perhaps you could say, "You can talk with Tech Support or you might want to ask Ted for help. He's a genius at that kind of stuff."

Instead of assigning a teacher to an extracurricular activity, perhaps you could ask, "Rita, you could be in charge of the debate team this year, or head up the Junior Achievement club. Which do you prefer?"

This may seem minor, but it can make a big difference in whether people feel in charge of their circumstances or a victim of their circumstances.

Are We Having Fun Yet?

"There's no such thing as fun for the whole family."
—Jerry Seinfeld

Actually, there is such a thing as fun for the whole family, as long as the whole family's in on the fun. This was marvelously illustrated by a seminar participant who seemed particularly fascinated with the insight that even when we're acting in the best interests of the group, the group may not appreciate our leadership if we're the only one making all the decisions.

He said, "I wish I'd known this last year. My oldest son was going away to college in the fall, and I realized if we were ever going to take that driving vacation we had always talked about, it was going to have to be that summer. I called AAA to get maps and spent hours studying all the possible routes across America, designing the itinerary, and making reservations.

"The big day finally came. We picked up our motor home in California and started driving. We hadn't gone ten miles when my youngest daughter asked, 'So, Dad, when do we get to Disneyland?' I explained we weren't going there because it was too crowded in July and wasn't worth waiting in the long lines.

"She couldn't believe it. 'We're half an hour away from Disneyland, and we're not going?' I explained that we had to go to the Grand Canyon in two days, so we had a lot of driving to get under our belts. Suffice it to say, she wasn't very happy with my decision and grumbled about it for the rest of the day."

He continued, "Have any of you ever driven east out of Los Angeles on a summer afternoon? All we could see from horizon to horizon was hot, dry desert with heat waves shimmering up from the melting asphalt. We couldn't wait to get to our campground so we could cool off in the swimming pool. We arrived after twelve hours of driving, hooked up our

RV, and walked over to the pool with great anticipation . . . only to discover it had a crack in the bottom and not one drop of water. Argghh!

"After another long day of driving, we finally got to the Grand Canyon, and couldn't find anywhere to park our large Winnebago. After driving around and around, I finally gave up and left it on the side of the road. At that point, I didn't care if it got towed. They could have the darn thing.

"We walked over to the side of the 'Big Ditch.' My youngest daughter took one look, turned to me in disgust, and wailed, '*We missed Disneyland for this*?!'

The father continued with his vacation vignette: "It went downhill from there. The next day, all I heard were complaints from the backseat drivers. 'Are we there yet?' 'Can't we stop?' 'How much longer?'

"I got more and more resentful. Didn't they understand I had spent hours preparing this trip? Didn't they realize I took three weeks off work so we could have this time together? Didn't they appreciate all the time I had poured into planning this? Finally, in frustration, I grabbed my auto club map, ripped it in half, threw it up in the air, and said, '*I give up*. You *plan the vacation*!'

"And that's what we did. We divvied up the days. My daughter had a day, my son had a day, my wife had a day, and I had a day. On 'your' day, you were in charge. The two rules were we had to get to that day's destination by 7 P.M. and we had to stay within our agreed spending limit. If it was your day and you wanted to sleep in, everyone slept in. If we were driving along and you saw a live snake show and you wanted to go to the live snake show, we all went to the live snake show.

"You know what? We had the best time together as a family we've ever had. And, I finally realized why they weren't enjoying their vacation. It wasn't *their* vacation. It was *my* vacation."

Educators Don't Dictate, They Draw Out

"The mediocre teacher tells. The good teacher explains. The
superior teacher demonstrates. The great teacher inspires."
—William Arthur Ward

I have retold this man's story many times, and it never fails to get a reaction. Many of us have been there, done that. We've put a lot of time and effort into organizing something, and instead of gratitude, all we got were gripes. We chair a fundraising committee and donate count-less hours to generating revenue, only to have people second-guess our every decision.

From now on, understand that people will often be ungrateful if we're in control of the situation and they're not. This relegates them to being backseat drivers and they're sure to grumble about what they think we should have done. If we can more equitably distribute control by offering options and letting people pick the one they prefer, or by out-lining parameters and letting them come up with the plan, they'll feel like it's *their* decision.

Teaching Is about Facilitating Autonomy

"We learn best through self-discovery." —Socrates

A student activities advisor who read this book in advance told me, "This chapter really captures the essence of what it means to be a teacher. It's so much easier to do things ourselves. Whether it's working on the yearbook or building a float for homecoming, I could finish it faster and better. However, that defeats the purpose. Our job as teachers isn't to do it ourselves. It's to help our students learn how to do it for themselves.

"One of the biggest lessons I've learned is that I don't help my students by *helping* my students." She hastened to add, "It's not that I ignore their requests for assistance or abandon a student who's in need. It's just that if they run into a problem and I solve it for them, guess what they're going to do the next time they run into a problem? If I rescue them and take care of all their troubles, how are they ever going to learn how to be self-sufficient and make good decisions?

"In college I learned about the Socratic Method of teaching. A good teacher doesn't say, '2 + 2 = 4. 4 + 4 = 8.' A good teacher asks, 'What's 2 + 2? What's 4 + 4?' To the largest degree possible, instead of outlining explicit instructions on exactly how to do something (which relegates students to simply following orders and staying unengaged), I try to guide them by asking questions. Instead of telling them not to use col-ored crepe paper because it makes a terrible mess if it gets wet, I'll ask, 'What do you think might happen if it rains during the parade?' That inspires them to start thinking and learning for themselves, which is my goal as a teacher."

Abraham Lincoln said, "You cannot help men permanently by doing for them what they could and should do for themselves." Exactly. Next time you're about to take charge of something, ask yourself how you can share control instead of take control. That is the true mark of a leader and an educator.

Tongue Fu! Tip for Teens

Many high school students tell me this is what they like least about being a teenager. As one of my son's friends put it, "Everyone tells me what to do, what not to do, when to do it, when not to do it. Sometimes, I just want to scream, 'Leave me alone.' That's why I can't wait to go away to college. Finally, I'll get to make my own decisions."

I told him, "Would you like to know a way you could get at least some control over your life?"

He said, "You know the answer to that!"

I suggested, "Do what one young man did. Eric's parents had a rule that he couldn't watch TV until he finished his homework. The 'problem' was, Eric loved to watch ESPN's SportsCenter from 6 to 7 P.M., but he didn't get home from practice until just before 6—which meant he never had his homework done and never got to watch his favorite show. He sat down with his parents one night and 'negotiated' a deal. He said, 'I know what you care about is that I keep my 3.6 average. Can we try something out on a probationary basis? I promise to maintain my grades, however I get to do my homework on my own time. If, at the end of the quarter, my grades slip, we go back to our old system. Okay?' His folks agreed to Eric's suggestion because it made so much sense."

If you want more autonomy, make your parents a deal they can't refuse. Identify the results they want (whether it's a lawn being mowed or a certain GPA) and agree to deliver that, with the understanding that the process—how and when you fulfill your commitment—is up to you. You get more control and they get the results they want. That's a win-win.

Action Plan of Don't Take Control, Share Control

You're the FFA advisor (Future Farmers of America) and you're planning the students' trip to the state fair. You've been doing this for twenty years and could do it in your sleep; however, the students have requested more "ownership" and want to participate more actively in the planning. What do you do?

Words to Lose	Words to Use
You take charge of the planning just like you've always done. *"I've made reservations for us at the Executive Inn. It's only a mile away from the fairgrounds."*	You involve students in the process. *"Here are a list of five hotels we've stayed at before. Who'd like to contact them?"*
You make all the arrangements by yourself. *"I've put up a list of who's going to be competing in showmanship."*	You share control by posing options and letting them pick. *"Let's vote for who will represent us in showmanship."*
You continue to make all the decisions because you "know best." *"Here's the schedule for cleaning the barns. Make sure you're on time for your shift."*	You know it's best to give others some autonomy. *"Please agree upon a schedule for keeping the barns clean and post it so we all know when our shift is."*
You feel resentful because no one appreciates all the effort you've put into organizing this. *"I'm tired of all this griping. Don't you understand I stayed up until midnight to put all this together?!"*	People are happier because decisions are being made *by* them instead of happening *to* them. *"What else can we do to make this the best state fair we've ever been part of?"*

"Where laws end, tyranny begins."

—William Pitt

Lay Down the Laws

C an you imagine what it would be like driving on a busy city street with no traffic lights, road signs, or crosswalks? It'd be chaos. No one would be safe.

Think about it. Why is it we can drive down a busy two-lane highway and have a car whiz by us going 60 mph, yet we don't even blink? It's because there are rules of the road and we trust people to follow them. That's why we can sail through a green light at an intersection and not worry about someone crashing into the side of our car. We're confident other drivers will obey the traffic signals.

Rules of the road make it possible for us to coexist safely even when we're traveling at high speeds in different directions. There are rules in football games: you can't hit a quarterback after he's released the ball. There are rules in boxing: you can't hit below the belt or after the bell.

Yet, surprisingly, there are often no rules in human relationships. We get married and are supposed to live together "happily ever after"—however, we never agree to rules that will increase the likelihood of that happening. We chair a meeting to discuss a controversial policy; yet we don't set up groundrules to make sure it doesn't deteriorate into a free-for-all. As a result, people interrupt each other, monopolize conversations, and call each other names. With no standards of behavior established, no wonder people run amok.

Set Up Rules to Curb Unruly Behavior

"If men were angels, no government would be necessary."
—James Madison

Years ago, the Hawaii State Department of Education asked me to chair the Volunteer Committee for its annual conference. This day-long event brought together students, teachers, administrators, parents, and DOE officials from around the island to discuss issues facing public schools.

The agenda included several emotionally charged issues, including a controversial proposal to have mandatory drug and sex education. At the end of the day, we all gave each other a standing ovation. Participants unanimously agreed that the issues had been thoroughly addressed and everyone had an equal opportunity to air his or her views. While individual suggestions may not have carried the day, the attendees, as a whole, felt the process was fair, and they were willing to support the consensus outcome.

Why were we able to achieve such success when, in the past, this annual conference had turned into a day-long shouting match? Because we arranged to have each focus group facilitated by a trained mediator who outlined groundrules at the outset and made sure everyone observed them. One of the mediators approached me afterward and said, "I just received the ultimate compliment. Our most opinionated participant stopped on his way out the door, shook my hand, praised me for keeping our session on track, and pronounced, 'You were pleasantly unpleasant.'"

I've always liked that characterization. As chairperson, we may need to be "pleasantly unpleasant" when enforcing the groundrules. It isn't always easy to grab the floor from someone who's ardently expounding his heartfelt view. Interrupting a heated discussion to get the focus back on solutions may initially ruffle feathers, yet the results are worth it. Invariably, group members will appreciate the fact that *everyone's* rights are being honored, instead of the rights of an aggressive few.

We've Got to Start Meeting Like This

"We need a twelve-step group for compulsive talkers. We're going to call it On Anon Anon." —Paula Poundstone

From now on, whether you're conducting a faculty meeting, a PTA meeting, whatever, you can increase the likelihood that it will be worthwhile for all involved by establishing, discussing, and posting the following rules at the beginning.

Posting the rules in large lettering where they can be seen by everyone is important, because if someone gets out of line, you can simply point to the sign and say, "Remember, we all agreed it's in our best interests to follow these rules." That softens what could be taken as a rebuke and keeps your remarks neutral so a confrontation doesn't arise between you and this individual.

Groundrules for Productive Meetings

1. **One person speaks at a time.** If someone interrupts or if several people start a side conversation, enforce this rule with these methods:
   - Look at the original speaker, hold your hand up toward them, and say in a firm yet warm voice, "Excuse me, [name of speaker], let's wait until we have everyone's attention." Be sure to finish your statement with a downward inflection. If your voice goes up at the end, you may sound tentative and the interrupter won't feel compelled to cooperate.
   - Do *not* look at the interrupter. If you look at the interrupter, everyone else will too. That will either 1) give the interrupter the floor along with everyone's attention, or 2) embarrass him in front of his peers and he'll resent you for causing him to lose face. Neither result is helpful.
   - If the interrupter continues talking, continue to look at the speaker and repeat your call to order in a louder, more commanding voice.
   - Only after it's completely quiet do you give the floor back to the speaker with a flourish of your hand and a "Thank you, [name of speaker], please proceed. You were saying. . . ."
   - Having facilitated and emceed hundreds of retreats and conferences over the last twenty-five-plus years, I can promise that if you enforce this rule immediately and consistently early on, you can establish a positive precedent that carries through the entire program. Honoring the speaker's right to be heard will

become the norm, and people will pay courteous attention to each other instead of thoughtlessly barging in whenever they have something to say.

2. **Participants can speak only once on each agenda item until everyone who wants to contribute has done so.** This rule prevents forceful personalities from dominating the discussion and turning it into a monologue while shy participants hold back because they're uncomfortable wresting the conversational ball away from opinionated peers.

   How do you enforce this? If Nora speaks out of turn (before other attendees have contributed their comments), put your hand up and say, "Nora, we want to hear what you have to say. First, let's find out what the rest of the group thinks about this. Wayne? Teresa? Your thoughts?"

3. **Participants can speak for up to two minutes at a time (or substitute your own reasonable time limit).** While this may seem unnecessarily strict, it serves an important purpose. My mom taught me, "That which can be done at any time rarely gets done at all." Unless there's a time limit, people have no reason to speak succinctly. They will repeat themselves, ramble, and wax eloquent (or not so eloquent) while the rest of the group goes to Tahiti in their minds.

   In their classic book, *Elements of Style*, authors Strunk and White say, "Vigorous writing is concise." Vigorous speaking is also concise. A two-minute maximum can transform boring bull sessions into fascinating, fast-paced meetings. Ask, "Who would like to be timekeeper?" Appointing someone else to keep track of time frees you to keep the conversation moving forward. Ask the timekeeper to give fifteen-second "warnings" so people know when to start wrapping up their thoughts. When time is up, gently but firmly interrupt and say, "Thanks, Brad, for that suggestion. Who else has an idea about this?"

Establish Standards of Behavior

"I have my standards. They may be low, but I have them."
—Bette Midler

Three additional rules can ensure peaceful deliberation of even the most volatile topics, and can make sure people behave in ways that help accomplish the group's goals.

Groundrules for Productive Meetings, continued

4. **Name-calling and negating other people's opinions are not allowed**. It's not permissible to say, "That's a lie" or "That's not how it happened." Telling someone he's wrong or she's a hypocrite is a surefire way to start a fight. You can diplomatically disagree by using an "I" statement: "I don't agree with that" or "I have a different impression of what took place that night." See the difference? Using the word "I" is a way to state your position without attacking the other person. It's a way for everyone to "have their say" and get their opinion on the table in a constructive, nonconfrontational manner.

5. **Voices need to be kept low.** This may seem like a rather subjective rule, but it serves a very important purpose. Stanley Horowitz observed, "Nothing lowers the level of conversation more than raising the voice." He's right. The louder people talk, they less they listen. The higher the volume, the higher the emotions. Speaking in a normal tone helps people interact objectively. You can model this by keeping your voice calm and by speaking in measured tones. If tempers start to flare and the volume starts increasing, say, "Okay everyone, let's all take a deep breath and start again. We can hear each other talking at this level. No need to shout."

6. **Focus on the action to be taken instead of dwelling on the past.** For meetings to be worthwhile, they must accomplish something tangible. For that to happen, the discussion cannot be allowed to deteriorate into blaming, shaming, finger-pointing, and faultfinding. If the meeting grinds down into a gripe session, put your hand up (even if you're not in charge of the meeting) and say, "It's obvious there are strong feelings about this issue, and we've got a half hour left and eight more items on our agenda. Can we table discussion on this for now, and move forward so we can accomplish our other objectives? If we have time left over at the end of the meeting, we can come back to this."

Establish "Behavior Boundaries"

"If we don't stand for something, we'll fall for anything."
—Ann Landers

My Aunt Carol was a gifted kindergarten teacher. She was loved by her students—and it wasn't because she was easy on them. I had an opportunity to visit her classroom one time and was impressed with how well behaved these energetic five-year-olds were. I asked why these children gave her such willing, instantaneous obedience and she said it was because she set up her expectations and "behavior boundaries" the first day of class.

"If you start strict, you can loosen up as time goes by—but if you start off lax, you'll be playing catch up the rest of the year.

"Within the first hour on the first day, I call them to attention and say, 'Class, when I clap my hands three times, there's to be absolute silence. Let's practice.'" She would do that until everyone, and I mean everyone, got it right. "Right" meant not one giggle or whisper. Within minutes, she said, the children would shush each other as soon as she clapped her hands, and she never had to ask for their attention twice.

Then they would practice standing up on a certain hand signal (as when they were going to salute the flag) and lining up at the door at a particular hand signal (as when they were going to recess).

Aunt Carol didn't believe in wishy-washy rules that were enforced one day and not the next, applied to one child and not the other. She believed that, "Children like to be well led, and they like to be well mannered. They welcome boundaries because boundaries give them clarity instead of confusion. They know what's expected of them and they feel safer."

Are you wondering what this has to do with Tongue Fu!? Many times when people aren't getting along, it's not because they're "bad." It's because no one has set up behavioral boundaries. Do yourself and the people around you a favor by laying down the laws so everyone can coexist cooperatively instead of conversation deteriorating into backbiting and bad-mouthing.

Are you thinking, "Too late. I'm already half way through the school year"? Actually, it's not too late, as long as you claim a "mea culpa" (Latin for "my fault"). Simply inform your group, "Mea culpa. I should have established groundrules at the beginning of this meeting, and I failed to do so. To ensure that we accomplish our goals and operate cooperatively and productively, we're going to establish our groundrules and standards of behavior now." As they say, better late than never.

Tongue Fu! Tip for Teens

One high school student told me he'd stopped inviting friends over to his house because they kept trashing it. "We live on a lake. It's fun having everyone over to hang out on our dock, but I got tired of cleaning up the mess they left. My mom used to buy pizzas and sodas for us, but everyone threw their cups and plates all over the place. I got disgusted that nobody picked up after themselves."

I asked him, "Did you ever have groundrules?"

He looked at me blankly. "What do you mean by groundrules?"

I said, "Your friends can't be faulted for not obeying rules they didn't know existed. Why not give them one more chance? This time, when you issue the invitation, let them know that whether or not they get asked back depends on whether your backyard looks *better than* it did when they arrived. Ask them, 'Do you like hanging out at our house? If you do, then it's in your best interests to take five minutes to clean up before you go so we can keep having these parties.' Then, hold your friends accountable by putting out the garbage cans in advance and giving everyone a big black trash bag before they leave."

Guess what? It worked. Are you upset with someone because he or she has not been treating you with the respect you deserve? Is there a chance this person doesn't even know his/her behavior is bothering you? If you don't like how someone's treating you, it's your responsibility to make sure they know what your expectations are. They can't honor boundaries they haven't been told about.

Action Plan for Lay Down the Laws

You're the music teacher in charge of a Madrigal singing group that will be performing in a regional competition in a coastal city the same time as "Beach Week." Several parents have expressed concern about their teens being in this town when there will be a lot of carousing and underage drinking. What do you do?

Words to Lose	Words to Use
You call a meeting to discuss everyone's concerns, and it quickly gets out of control. *"I've heard the kids are planning to sneak out and buy booze and hit the dance clubs."*	You call a meeting and establish groundrules at the outset. *"Let's agree to follow these rules so we treat each other with respect."*
Since no standards of behavior were established, people start faultfinding and finger-pointing. *"Your son's the ring-leader. He's the one telling everyone which clubs don't check I.D."*	Since standards of behaviors were set up, people focus on what action could be taken. *"How can we make sure the kids have chaperones with them at all times?"*
The conflict gets worse because participants become more and more emotional and distraught. *"This isn't safe. I'm not letting my daughter go on the trip."*	The controversy gets addressed and resolved because the discussion is kept productive. *"Okay, so we're taking ten parents and there will be an adult in each room."*

"Half the world is composed of people who have something to say and can't, and the other half who have nothing to say and keep saying it."

—Robert Frost

Tactfully Terminate Monologues

Would you like to know what to do if someone won't stop talking?

In previous chapters, we've discussed the importance of listening, of putting ourselves in the other person's shoes, and of giving people our empathic, undivided attention.

Those are important steps to creating a climate of cooperation; however, there are times when people are taking advantage of our largesse and it's appropriate to courteously close the conversation and move on. There are also times when someone's one-sided, long-winded remarks are contributing to, or causing, a conflict. The next time someone is holding forth at everyone's expense, don't suffer in silence. Use the following six "Tactful Termination" steps to reestablish an equity in the views being expressed.

Six Steps to Tactful Termination

1. **Determine if the needs being met are out of balance.** Picture an old-fashioned scale. See the person talking and their needs on

one side of the scale and you and your needs on the other side of the scale.

If someone's been talking to you for twenty minutes, their needs are probably being met. How about your needs? How about the needs of the two students who have been waiting to talk to you? How about the needs of the teachers who are waiting for you to show up at the faculty meeting? How about those e-mails that aren't getting answered because this one individual is holding you up?

You can see that this scale is out of balance. It's tilted to the advantage of the person who has been monopolizing our time and attention. We're serving their needs; however, it's at the expense of our needs. In this case, it's not selfish to diplomatically bring this overlong conversation to a close, it's smart. It's appropriate to bring the scale back in balance so we can serve the needs of many people instead of just one.

Most of us have been taught that it's impolite to interrupt. We've been told that cutting in is unacceptable under any circumstances. It's time for us to update that perception. There are times it's appropriate to let people vent and get things off their chest. If, however, people are taking advantage of your courtesy, or if you perceive that continued listening would give them an undeserved pulpit that serves no one, it's appropriate to cut their comments short. If, in your judgment, this other person isn't going to stop talking on his or her own, and if there are other people's needs that take precedence, then it's not rude for you to interrupt—it's right.

2. **Interrupt by saying their name.** Do not send subtle signals in the hopes this person will take a hint and put a sock in it. Tapping your foot or glancing pointedly at your watch probably won't get through. If they're insensitive enough to blab on ad infinitum, they'll probably ignore polite hints to give someone else a chance to speak. If you start talking over them, they'll probably protest, "Hey, I'm not finished," and begin again, louder this time. When people hear their name, they pause, and that will give you a chance to start bringing the conversation to a close.

3. **Summarize what they've said.** This is the key to ending someone's soliloquy without offending them. If you interrupt and immediately begin sharing your point of view, they'll be affronted.

It will be clear that you cut them off to have your own say. If you instead paraphrase what they've said, they'll know you've understood the gist of what they were trying to get across.

4. **Start wrapping up with "As soon as" or "I wish."** If there's something you can do to improve their situation, say "As soon as we hang up, I'm going to get in touch with the principal and bring this to her attention" or "As soon as we finish talking, I'm going to get in touch with his parents and let them know about their son's bullying."

    Letting the other person know what you're going to do—as soon as the conversation is over—motivates them to stop talking so you can take action on their matter sooner rather than later.

    If they're just going on and on because they're upset, because they like to hear themselves talk, or because they're not aware of your other priorities, say "I wish." "Susan, I wish I had more time to hear about the bullying that's taking place on the playground, but I have a faculty meeting right now. Could I please have your phone number and call you tonight so we can discuss this in more detail?" Using the words "I wish" softens the fact that you're terminating the conversation, and lets them know you do want to hear what they have to say.

5. **Finish with finality and a friendly phrase.** Pleasant phrases such as "I *appreciate* you bringing this to my attention" or "I *look forward* to talking with you tonight" offset any perception of abruptness. Make sure your voice ends with warm, downward inflection. If you trail off tentatively or end with an "okay?" you'll throw the conversational ball right back in their court and they'll probably pick it up and run with it again. Phrases such as "I'm *glad* we had a chance to discuss this" or "*Thank you* for telling me about what happened" will provide a positive emotional context to your conversation so they don't perceive you're coldly cutting them off.

6. **Use body language to diplomatically disengage.** If the other person insists on holding you spellbound, it's time to become more assertive. Standing up from your chair or taking a few steps backwards is a physical way of saying, "This conversation is over." You are literally and figuratively distancing yourself from the person and "breaking" the contact. Be sure to keep your eyes on theirs so they don't feel you're turning your back on them. Say something that lets them know you're not just walk-

ing away, you're headed to an appointment or to another obligation. Saying, "The bell's going to ring any minute. I better get
back to my class" is a way to wrap up graciously so they don't
feel summarily cut off.

Keep Discussions Time Efficient and Mutually Beneficial

"The misfortune in conversation is this: people go on without
knowing how to get off." —Samuel Johnson

One teacher told me, "It wasn't the students, parents, or fellow teachers who monopolized my time. It was my principal. Every time I went
into his office, I braced myself because I knew I was going to be in there
a l-o-n-g time. You've heard the line about the egoist who said, 'Enough
about me. What do *you* think of me?' That's him. I didn't think it was my
place to interrupt him; he's my boss! That scale of needs really clarified
things for me. I realized that sitting there and listening to him go on and
on wasn't helping either of us and it wasn't getting my work done.

"The Monday after your workshop, I needed to go into his office to
ask something. Sure enough, he started in. This time though, I didn't
just sit there and wait for him to take a breath so I could get a word in
edgewise. I interrupted and said, 'Al, I wish I had time to hear more
about your golf tournament, but I've got thirty papers to grade by tomorrow morning [again, and/but]. Congratulations again on getting 'closest
to the pin.' That must have been exciting. I better get moving now if I'm
going to have these finished by first period. See you tomorrow.'

She continued, "At first, I thought he was going to be offended, however, he doesn't seem to mind when I wrap things up. I just comment on
something he's said, so he knows I've been listening, and then let him
know I've got to get going to finish some project. You know what I've
come to realize? He doesn't mean to be a bore; it's just that he loves an
audience and doesn't know when to stop."

People Can't Monopolize Your Time
Unless You Let Them

"I can't give you the formula for success. I can for failure. Try to
please everyone." —Bill Cosby

Are you thinking this is a blazing attack of the obvious? Perhaps so, but countless educators have told me what a problem this is for them. Columnist Abigail Van Buren even featured this complaint in a column. A teacher wrote in to ask what she could do about a needy friend who called a minimum of four times a week and rattled on for at least an hour each time. The teacher said she worked with people ten hours a day and the last thing she wanted to do when she got home was talk on the phone. Despite her hints about how "tired" she was, her friend continued to bend her ear. She said, "I don't want to hurt my friend's feelings but it's gotten to the point I don't even want to answer my own phone anymore."

Abby told the woman, "No one can walk all over you if you don't lie down first." She went on to suggest that this teacher tell her friend outright that she needed her evenings free to recharge her batteries, and that they should make some arrangements to connect on the weekend.

Kudos. Abby's advice wasn't cold-hearted, it was balanced! She wasn't suggesting this teacher ignore her friend altogether—she was simply pointing out that taking her every phone call was persistently putting her friend's needs before her own, and that wasn't fair either. Remember, people can't "talk" all over you unless you let them.

Tongue Fu! Tip for Teens

One teen told me, "I've stopped hanging out with Steffie because all she ever does is talk about herself. It gets so annoying." I asked her, "Did you ever tell Steffie how you felt?" "I shouldn't have to tell her!" she said indignantly.

I said, "Do you ever watch the TV sitcom *Friends*?" She looked at me like I was one taco short of a combination plate. "What's that got to do with anything?"

I explained, "In one of the episodes, Phoebe is carrying on about something her brother did. Joey finally gets tired of her whining and asks, "Have you told him how you feel?"

Phoebe says primly, "Yes." Then she admits, "Well, not out loud."

Many of us complain about someone's behavior to our friends, our parents, everyone *but* the person who is bothering us. That isn't going to change anything!

If someone has done something that hurt your feelings or caused you to back off, do that person and yourself a favor. Tell them how you feel—out loud and to their face. They may not know they did something that chased you away. Instead of expecting them to read your mind, take responsibility for bringing the problem to their attention.

Reapproach your friend, let her know you think things have been a little one-sided, and you'd like to continue to be friends as long as this changes. She may reject your request outright, or she may apologize and promise to do better.

Anticipate that she'll fall back into her old habits. Next time she gets "me-deep" in conversation, interrupt and say, "My turn." or "This is where you ask, 'And how was *your* day?'"

Give her the benefit of the doubt. She may not have had anyone teach her how to hold balanced conversations. Promise yourself you won't suffer in silence while she talks on and on, meanwhile silently deciding not to have anything to do with her. Hold her accountable for two-way conversations. If she continues to show no interest in making this a win–win friendship despite your best efforts to create one, THEN move on. Give her a chance to be more courteous first.

Action Plan for Tactfully Terminate Monologues

You're a college counselor who has given your home phone number to students so they can have someone to turn to in time of need. Lately, several have been having a rough time (they're homesick, don't like their professors, or are confused about their major), and they've been calling almost every night. Your heart goes out to them, but you're getting burned out because you don't have any free time at night to recharge your batteries. What do you do?

Words to Lose	Words to Use
You think only of their needs and continue to listen.	You think of the scale of needs and decide to keep them balanced.
"I'm so tired I can hardly keep my eyes open, but she's going through such a hard time."	*"I want to help her, and I need to get to sleep if I want to function tomorrow."*

Words to Lose	Words to Use
You selflessly focus on what they want, and get more and more burned-out. *"It feels like I'm on the job fourteen hours a day. I don't know how much longer I can keep this up."*	You focus on what's fair for everyone involved and choose to listen for ten minutes and then bring the conversation to a close. *"Five more minutes and I need to wrap this up for tonight and get to bed."*
You wait for her to stop talking so you can get a word in edgewise, and she never does. *"My gosh, she's been carrying on for thirty minutes now."*	You say their name to tactfully interrupt and summarize what they've been saying. *"So, Cindy, I understand you want to switch majors."*
You expect her to read your mind and know you're tired of the one-way conversation. *"Doesn't she realize I have a family and responsibilities of my own? When am I supposed to get some time off?"*	You wrap up the conversation with an action statement and with warm words. *"Tell you what. I've got time tomorrow at 10 A.M. for an appointment. How about coming to my office then and we'll talk."*

22

"Being kind doesn't mean one needs to be a mat."

—Maya Angelou

Diplomatically Say "No"

A recurring theme of this book is that it is in everyone's best interests to be cordial and compassionate. As Angelou points out though, that doesn't mean becoming a doormat and allowing people to take advantage of our good will.

There are times it's appropriate to turn down requests and not "go along," and a key issue is, "How can we do that fairly and firmly, without jeopardizing our job or relationships?"

A teacher told me, "I'm like that character in the musical who sings, 'I can't say no.' You've heard the advice about giving assignments to the busiest person because you know the job will get done? That's me. I'm involved in so many activities, I can hardly keep them straight. I'm running on empty, but every time I pledge to cut back, someone begs me to take on another project. I've just been asked to chair the program committee for our annual Teachers Institute Day. I don't want to leave them in a lurch, but my husband and I hardly see each other anymore. Help!"

Picture the Scale of Needs to Determine Whose Needs Are Being Met

"There are three possible broad approaches to the conduct of interpersonal relations. The first is to consider one's self only

and ride roughshod over others. The second is always to put others before one's self. The third approach is the golden mean. The individual places himself first and takes others into account."
—Joseph Wolpe

The key to resolving the dilemma of when it's appropriate to say no is to make this intangible issue tangible. Instead of battling it out in our head, which just causes us to become more confused, we want to put this abstract matter down on paper so we see it in black and white. This makes it easier for us to make an objective decision.

The way to do this is to picture the old-fashioned scale that we discussed in the previous chapter, and then take the following steps:

1. Assign one side of the scale to the person who is asking you to do something. This side also stands for the other people and responsibilities in your world.
2. Assign the other side of the scale to yourself.
3. Now think back over your history with the "outside world" and with yourself—and write down who's been getting "yes's" and "their way" over the last year.
4. See the scale at the right to visualize how it might look if you have been consistently giving other people what they want and not speaking up or spending time on what you want. Understand that if the scale has been persistently out of balance, with you serving everyone's else's interests and not your own, it is not selfish for you to say no to this request—it is smart. If you can see that you've been thinking only of yourself, then perhaps it's time to think of others and say "yes" to this request.

Healthy Relationships Keep the Needs Being Met Balanced

"Selfishness is not living as one wishes to live—it is always asking others to live as one wishes to live." —Oscar Wilde

One of the fundamental concepts of Tongue Fu! is that the key to creating healthy, happy relationships is to keep the needs being met. . .

in balance. This is true whether it's a relationship between a parent and a child, a husband and a wife, a company and its customers, a principal and her staff, a teacher and his students.

If we consistently think only of what we need, consider only how we feel, indulge only in what we want to do, the scale will be tipped in our favor and indicate that we're acting *selfishly*—without regard to others.

On the other hand, if we always put our responsibility to others and the "world" first, if we only consider what others think, if we always give in to what they want, the scale will be skewed in their favor and we will be acting *selflessly.*

Neither extreme state is healthy. When the Relationship Scale of Needs is persistently lopsided, one side will feel unnoticed, undervalued, or taken advantage of, and it's only a matter of time before this causes conflict, dissatisfaction, or unhappiness that undermines and jeopardizes the relationship.

Another fundamental concept of Tongue Fu! is that we don't wait for or expect other people to look after OUR best interests. It would be nice if that happened, and it would mean we're fortunate enough to be dealing with fair-minded, magnanimous individuals; however, we don't naively count on others to initiate action on our behalf.

Take Responsibility for Keeping Your Relationship Equitable

"I like things to happen; and if they don't happen, I like to make them happen." —Winston Churchill

Each of us needs to take responsibility for keeping our own Scale of Needs in balance—if we do, we can live or work with other people in satisfying harmony instead of stressful hostility. If everyone took responsibility for keeping their Scale of Needs in balance, we could eliminate much of the over-the-top, "me-first" behavior—and the silent, long-suffering, "you-first" mentality—that perpetuates up-down, victimizing, or victimized relationships.

I suggested the teacher previously quoted jot down all the activities she was doing for other people on one side of the scale, and all the activities she was doing purely for her own reasons on the other side of the scale. First, record all the committees she'd chaired, the after-hours activities she'd participated in, the meetings she'd attended on one side—and then move to the other side of the scale.

How was her health? Was she exercising and getting the sleep she needed? How much time was she spending with family and friends? How about hobbies and special interests? What was she doing for fun? Listing her activities on their respective side of the scale could illuminate whether she was 1) spending her life the way *she* wanted, 2) spending her life the way *other people* wanted, or the golden mean 3) spending her life in a *balance* between what she wanted, needed, and deserved, and what others wanted, needed, and deserved.

The long list of community and school activities on one side of the scale compared to the paltry list of personal activities on "her" side of the scale made it clear that her life was not "her own" and the scale was seriously out of balance.

She said, "When I was asked to help with Teacher Institute Day, I felt guilty even thinking about turning them down. I was about to cave under their pressure and say yes, even though it was the last thing I wanted to do. Taking a few minutes to chart my scale of needs on paper was a lifesaver. As soon as I 'saw' my history of serving everyone but myself, I realized it was time to carve out some time for myself. Now the question is, how can I say no without alienating them?"

Five Ways to Say No Fairly and Firmly

"Do you have 'No' power or do you have no power?"
—Sonya Friedman

Good question. From now on, if you've figured out through the Scale of Needs that it's appropriate to say "no," here's how to do so without risking your friendships.

1. **Say no and yes.** Turn down this particular request and suggest an alternative that's more on your terms. Say, "I appreciate your offer, and I won't be able to do that, however I will be glad to. . . ." Perhaps this teacher could explain she's not in a position to chair the committee, however she would be glad to sug-

gest and contact a keynote speaker who would get the program off to a great start. Or, she could say no to chairing the committee, however she'd be glad to meet with them once and share her lessons learned from her previous years of organizing the event.

2. **Say no and solve their "problem" through other means.** Let them know that although you can't say yes to their specific request, you do have other ideas on how they can get their needs met. Perhaps this teacher could say, "I'm not available to chair the committee, however I'd like to recommend Paul. He's an excellent leader and would do a great job." That way, they're still getting what they want, a qualified chair, and the teacher is getting what she wants, free time.

3. **Say no graciously and without guilt.** If you've been giving, giving, giving, understand you have the right to say no without feeling bad about it. Although it would be nice to help out, it is not your responsibility to rescue them from their dilemma. Perhaps you could say with a smile, "I appreciate your offer, and my husband and I have promised to leave our evenings free so we can get reacquainted."

4. **Use Words to Use to keep your refusal diplomatic.** Whatever you say, be sure to avoid the trigger words "but" and "no way." If you say, "I know you need help, *but* there's *no way* I can chair this committee right now because I'm already overbooked," they will feel that you haven't even considered their request. Turning that into "I know you need help, *and* I wish I was in a position to pitch in. What I'd like to *suggest* is . . ." lets them know that you a) have thought this through, b) are doing your best to help out in a fair, balanced way, and c) are saying no for a good reason. They're much more likely to accept your refusal graciously because you're role-modeling graciousness.

5. **Keep it brief or they could give you grief.** The more succinct you are, the more convincing you'll be. The more reasons you give for your decision, the more apologetic you'll appear. Aggressive personalities may even try to take advantage of your perceived indecisiveness. If they persist, simply say with a smile, "My mind's made up," and then segue into another topic.

What If People Are Displeased by Your No?

"How I like to be liked, and what I do to be liked!" —Charles Lamb

This teacher wasn't yet convinced. She asked, "What if I do all that, and they still get mad at me?" Understand the connection between the compulsion to say yes and the need to please everyone.

In my book *Take the Bully by the Horns: Stop Unpleasant, Uncooperative, and Unethical People from Running and Ruining Your Life*, I dedicated a whole chapter to this issue of how the automatic urge to "go along to get along" can mask an unhealthy craving to please and a pathological need for approval.

The pleasers' motto is, "Is everybody happy?" Pleasers are quick to back off their opinions and needs with comments like "It doesn't matter" or "I don't mind," when it does matter and they do mind. Pleasers don't dare risk losing people's affection, so they say yes instead of no even when they don't want to be in charge of the third-grade bake sale—again.

A questionnaire entitled Who Am I Trying to Please and Why? on pages 113 and 114 of that book can help you determine whether you're saying yes for the right or wrong reasons.

Ask for Privacy So You Can Gain Perspective

"If you don't run your own life, someone else will."
—John Atkinson

If you have a history of wanting to please others, the best thing to do is to institute a policy that you will never again *spontaneously* agree to anything that requires time, money, or attention. If you traditionally collapse under coercion only to later lament, "What did I get myself into?" vow to yourself that you will only say yes to additional time-consuming responsibilities *after* you've had privacy to think things through.

Negotiators know that people make concessions they wouldn't ordinarily make when forced to give an immediate answer. That's why it's important to not let yourself be caught off guard. If you're mentally knocked off balance by someone's pressure (subtle or otherwise), you're more likely to give in.

That's why, the next time someone wants you to do something that will require time and effort, say, "I'd like some time to think about this," or "I want to check my calendar first. Let me review my other commitments and I'll get back to you with an answer first thing tomorrow."

Please note I'm not suggesting we avoid the issue. I'm suggesting we remove ourselves from the presence of someone who might be mentally crowding us and using verbal strong-arm tactics to convince us to concede. Only when we, literally and figuratively, *distance* ourselves from that person and give ourselves space to review the scale of needs will we be able to get some much-needed perspective on this issue.

If the other person is relentless and continues to press you to say yes, simply say, "Fine, if you have to have an answer right now, it's no." That will let them know it's not in their best interests to try to rush you. Or you can "name their game" by saying, "You're not trying to rush me into a decision, are you?" Not anymore, they're not!

You Have the Right to Say No

> "You can please most of the people some of the time, but some
> people you can't please none of the time." —Ziggy

One teacher told me, "This has been a difficult situation for me. Our school district requires that we spend eleven hours a month, uncompensated, in extracurricular activities. I understand that policy and willingly pitch in to help out with our after-school tutoring program. Past that though, I draw the line and do not participate in other school activities on evenings and weekends.

"Some teachers resent this and have told me to my face they feel I'm a 'time-card puncher' who does the minimum and nothing else. The thing is, I've got my own kids at home and every hour spent after school is an hour taken directly away from my time with them. It's not that I don't care for my students, it's just that I want to be there to see my own children grow up.

"Even though I was clear about this intellectually, it still hurt when other teachers turned their noses up when I would get up to leave and they would still be tutoring. I finally got over my guilt by reminding myself of Maggie Bedrosian's insight from her book *Life Is More Than Your To-Do List*. Her idea that 'Every time we say "no" to one thing we say "yes" to something else' helped me feel justified in my choice. I can't be all things to all people. Instead of frantically and futilely trying to be everything to everyone else and ending up being nothing to the people I love the most, I got clear that my time and energy are limited resources and it's not wrong to dedicate them to my own family."

A famous quote from the first-century philosopher Hillel the Elder asks, "If I am not for myself, who will be for me? If I am for myself alone, what am I? And if not now, when?" Those timeless words eloquently express the importance of serving ourselves *and* serving others. If we don't learn how to say no fairly and firmly, we'll pay the steep price of self-sacrifice. Be clear that you have a right and responsibility to maintain a fair balance in the needs being met and you'll find the courage to diplomatically reject requests that would compromise that.

Caveat

Please note that there are exceptions to this "right" to say no. Obviously, when we work for an organization and report to a supervisor, there are requests we have to say "yes" to, even though we would rather not. As a member of a union, there are rules we must follow even if we don't particularly agree with them. As a student, there are requirements that must be fulfilled, even if we don't want to.

The suggestions in this chapter are meant to be used when we have a *choice* of whether or not to say yes. There are responsibilities at school that "come with the territory." They may not be in writing, however, it's implied that these duties are an expected, "unpaid" part of the job.

One counselor told me, "We are supposed to attend every monthly PTSA meeting. It's not in our contract; however, our principal makes it very clear that we better be there." In one state, it's expected that teachers will get involved in political campaigns and "get out the vote" for candidates endorsed by their union.

If you're not sure whether a request is actually a requirement, ask, "Before I give an answer, could you please clarify if this is an option? If I said no, what would be the consequences?" It's better to know up front whether you have the "right of refusal"—otherwise, you might reject a request and suffer the penalties later.

Tongue Fu! Tip for Teens

First Lady Nancy Reagan suggested we "just say no" when asked if we want to drink, smoke, have sex, or do drugs.

You may be thinking, "Easier said than done. Adults don't understand how much peer pressure we're under to 'go along.'"

One teen told me, "My dad got a new job last year, so we had to move and I had to start a new high school my junior year. At first, it was hard to break in because I didn't know anyone. Finally, in the spring, I joined the baseball team and started making some friends. One night after practice, a few guys on the team came over to my house. We have a three-story condo and my room's on the bottom floor. We also have a playroom down there with my computer, a pool table, and a big TV. It's a fun place to hang out because we kind of have the place to ourselves and my friends can come in and out the back door.

"This became our Friday night ritual. Then, a couple of the guys started sneaking in beers, and some started sneaking in their girlfriends. Things started getting out of control. Every weekend, kids would ask if my parents were going to be out, and if they were, they'd want to come over. I don't drink, I guess I'm too scared of getting caught, but I didn't want to be 'uncool' so I kept giving in.

"Then, one weekend, my folks were out somewhere and my older brother came home from college and walked in on a party. Some kids were smoking and a couple were in my room with the door closed. He took one look around and asked me, 'Who *are* these kids?' I had to admit I didn't know half of them. He shook his head in disgust and went back upstairs.

"Later, after everyone had left and I'd gone to bed, he came into my room and said, 'Normally, I don't give advice, but I want to tell you something. You think all these kids like you because you're having these parties. Kevin, what they like is having a place where they can drink and smoke and have sex. *They're using you.*' Then he got up and left."

"His words hit me straight in my gut. I realized what he'd said was true. I decided I didn't want to be 'party central' anymore and started telling kids they'd have to find somewhere else to hang out. A few gave me a hard time, but I realized that anyone who gave me grief about this wasn't really my friend."

Wise young men, both of them. If you're being pressured by a friend to do something you don't want to do, remember, this person is not being your friend. Don't let people use you for their own purposes. Say "no" and be a friend to yourself.

Action Plan for Diplomatically Saying "No"

As a school secretary, you don't make much money. Because of your front office job, everyone on campus knows you and it seems you're constantly asked to contribute to one fundraiser or another. Today, it's 4-H, tomorrow it will be the chess club. The kids "only" want $10 or $20, and you want to support them, but you're on a very tight budget. What do you do?

Words to Lose	Words to Use
You feel pressured to say yes because you like to help others out. *"I'm short on cash, but I really do want to support your 5K walk."*	You picture the scale of needs to determine if you've been helping others at the expense of yourself. *"Give me a minute to see if I've got enough cash."*
You think only of what they want and give in to their pleading. *"Well, I can't afford this, but it's for a good cause."*	You see the scale is out of balance; it's time to say "no." *"Good luck with your fund drive, but I've given my allotted amount this week."*
The kids persist and you find yourself weakening under their pressure. *"Hey, don't make me out to be a mean person just 'cause I'm not contributing."*	You understand you have a right to say "no." *"I need to save this money so I can afford to pay for Alyssa's piano lessons.*
You get upset with yourself for not standing up for what's fair. *"I can't believe I gave in again. When am I going to grow a spine?"*	You say no and yes on your terms so it's a win-win. *"Tell you what. Come here first thing on Monday, and you'll get my $20 for next week."*

23

"Some act first, think afterward, and repent forever."

—Charles Simmons

Choose Your Battles so You Act Wisely, Not Rashly

Would you like to know how to think first and act afterward so you don't have to worry about repenting forever?

Just because we don't like how someone is behaving doesn't mean it's smart to speak up right then. What is smart is to consider all the influencing factors and possible consequences before "going forth into battle."

A teacher finally succeeded in getting pregnant after years of trying. She had a difficult eight months and spent the last few weeks at home flat on her back under doctor's orders. She gave birth to a healthy daughter, but developed an infection and ended up needing even more time to get back to full health. Her principal was generous about her extended maternity leave, even though it was exceedingly difficult finding a substitute who was qualified to take her class.

A week after returning to school, this teacher found out her position as advisor to the "It's Academic" team had been given to another teacher. She was incensed as she had taken the team to the state finals three years in a row and loved preparing the kids for the competitions.

She said she was ready to march into the principal's office and tell him exactly what she thought when a little voice in her head asked, "Is this good timing?" She realized the principal had been going to bat for her for the last four months, and it wouldn't be fair to give him grief after he had been so supportive all that time. Fortunately, she had the presence of mind to ask herself one of the key "Choose Your Battle" questions before putting her foot in her mouth.

To Speak or Not to Speak, That Is the Question

"Only a fool tests the depth of the water with both feet."
—African proverb

Think of a situation that is bothering you, a person who is not treating you "right," or a person who is not giving you what you want, need, and deserve.

Talk yourself through these Choose Your Battle criteria to determine whether you should speak—or forever hold your peace.

Eight Choose Your Battle Criteria

1. **Is it trivial?** Maybe a parent called you "honey," and you don't like being called "honey." Ask yourself, "Am I ever going to see this person again?" If not, perhaps you can afford to shrug this off and let it go. This issue does not affect world peace. It's what Hawaiians call "manini"—small fish.

2. **Is it a persistent concern?** What if this parent is volunteering in your classroom and you're going to be seeing her several times a week? What if she starts calling you "honey" every time she sees you? Now the stakes are higher. This is not a one-time thing; it's an ongoing concern. It may matter enough to speak to her at this point. Perhaps you could politely remind her of your full name and ask her to call you that so the children will follow suit.

3. **Is her behavior innocent or intentional?** She may have grown up in the South and calls everyone "honey." Perhaps she doesn't mean anything negative by it. In fact, she may be using it as an affectionate endearment. Or, maybe she's being deliberately condescending or patronizing. Try to determine whether the woman is doing this on purpose or by accident.

4. **What's the history of the situation?** Are there extenuating circumstances that explain or "excuse" the person's behavior? Maybe you don't like how she or he is treating you; however, the person is mentally challenged. Maybe you're unhappy with a situation, but you've already complained three times this week and you've worn out your welcome. Even if what you have to say is valid, the decision maker may not be listening anymore because you've worn out your goodwill credit.

5. **Can or will their behavior change?** Is this person motivated to act differently, or will your entreaties fall on "deaf ears?" Maybe this parent has been calling women "honey" all her life and has no intention of changing now. Maybe her attitude is, "This is the way I am. If you don't like it, tough." I saw some graffiti once that said, "Never try to teach a pig to sing. It's a waste of your time, and it annoys the pig." You may conclude that trying to persuade her to stop calling you "honey" is the equivalent of trying to teach a pig to sing.

6. **Is this good timing?** Teens are usually very intuitive about understanding the important role timing plays in decision making. They check out the expression on their mom or dad's face *before* they ask for the car keys, because they intuitively understand that whether or not they get them has a lot to do with what mood their parents are in. Remember, it's not whether you have a valid case, it's not whether what you're saying is true, it's whether the decision maker is in a mood to say yes.

7. **How am I contributing to this?** Before getting upset with someone because they're "mistreating" us, we need to look at ourselves to see what role we may have played in this. Jack Canfield said, "People treat us the way we teach them to treat us." Perhaps, as discussed in chapter 20, you didn't establish groundrules in the beginning and make clear to your volunteers that you'd like to be addressed as Ms. Baker to be consistent with what students call you.

8. **Would confronting this person result in a short-term win and a long-term loss?** Ask yourself, "If I go to the mat over this issue, what will happen? Could I win the battle and lose the war? Would it be better to overlook this minor issue in favor of a larger goal?" George Patton suggested, "Take calculated risks. This is

quite different from being rash." Maybe you anticipate that the price you'd pay for tackling this issue head-on is not worth the potential risk.

Put Your Mind in Gear before You Put Your Mouth in Motion

"The hardest thing to learn in life is which bridge to cross and which to burn." —David Russell

I don't agree with Mr. Russell that learning which battle to fight is the hardest thing to learn in life, but it certainly can be complex. At least considering these criteria can help you reach a decision you can live with.

This was the case with a group of school administrators who attended an all-day Tongue Fu! program. I had divided the audience into small groups so everyone would have a chance to swap notes and brainstorm possible resolutions to challenges they were facing. One principal was facing what seemed to be a no-win dilemma: "I have a teacher who's retired on the job. My hands are tied because of her tenure and because she's being protected by her union. I have documented reports from students and parents testifying to her incompetence. I've arranged counseling, hired a teacher's assistant, and monitored her classroom to no avail.

"She thinks I'm persecuting her and has vowed to file a grievance against me if I continue trying to have her removed. She's determined to stick it out these last two years and get her full benefits. What can I do?"

As you can imagine, this conundrum created quite a heated discussion. Participants suggested a variety of approaches, but the beleaguered principal claimed to have already tried all of them with no success. In the long run, the group reached a reluctant consensus. One of the administrators summed up their conclusion, "I've been in a similar situation and I know how frustrating it is. I eventually decided that going through the very lengthy, contentious process to fire this one underperforming teacher was not in the school's best interests."

He went on, "As leaders, we must make constant decisions about what constitutes the best use of our limited resources. My bottom-line decision was that it would have taken thousands of dollars and hundreds of hours to continue to pursue this issue. I decided it was a better use of our time to spend it on our many dedicated teachers who are doing their best to positively influence their students. My mentor told me, 'No one ever said being a principal is easy. That's why they pay us the big bucks.'" At this, everyone in the room laughed ruefully.

Know When to Hold 'Em, and When to Fold 'Em

"Wisdom is the anticipation of consequences." —Norman Cousins

You may be thinking, "That's an awful decision. What about the poor children in her class? Are they going to suffer because the principal doesn't have time to do the right thing? Is he just going to ignore her ineptitude?"

Believe me, these educators disliked this decision as much as you. In an ideal world, they never would have resorted to such a distressing and dissatisfying course of inaction. They would have taken the necessary steps to replace the teacher; her students would have received the quality instruction they deserved; and everything would have turned out copasetic.

In the real world, things don't always work out the way we'd like them to.

In the real world, there are times when none of the options available to us are appealing. If that's the case, consulting with others and talking ourselves through these Choose Your Battle criteria can help us make an informed decision—at least then we're making the best of a bad situation.

If you're facing a similarly complex dilemma and want a more in-depth questioning process, you might want to review pages 144 to 145 in *Take the Bully by the Horns*. The pages feature twenty questions that can help you decide whether to look away, walk away, or fire away. They can help you determine whether an issue is too petty to pursue or whether you're unwilling to "turn the other cheek" and want to take action. If you do decide to speak up, you'll learn how to increase receptivity to your pleas in our next chapter, "Five Rules of Ethical Persuasion."

Tongue Fu! Tip for Teens

Does it seem like your parents are always telling you "no"? Maybe you're going to the well too often. Understand that there's a negative cumulative impact of frequently asking for "favors." Some people (adults and older siblings included!) feel they have to say no every once in awhile, almost on principle. They don't want to be perceived as being "easy," so they say no just to remind you who's in charge. It's a way of reasserting control.

There's a way around this. Choose your battles. Save up your requests for something that really matters to you—and let your parents know what you're doing. Say, "Mom, [or Dad]. I'm going to stop pestering you all the time for more spending money. I'm going to wait until I really want something, and then I'll ask for my allowance. Okay?" They'll probably be impressed with, and motivated to reward, your mature approach.

If your older brother refuses to let you play on his computer, or your older sister refuses to let you borrow her clothes, apply the same principle. Say, "I know you get tired of me bugging you all the time. So, from now on, I'm only going to ask once a week to play on your computer." Or "I know I've been borrowing your clothes a lot lately. You're welcome to wear something of mine for a change." Now that's thinking before you speak and acting wisely instead of rashly.

Action Plan for Choose Your Battles so You Act Wisely, Not Rashly

It's the middle of winter and a blizzard is predicted. You turn on the TV in the morning and see your school has not declared a snow day. You bundle up your kids, put them on the bus, and head off to work. No sooner do you sit down at your desk then you get a call saying the school's closed and you need to pick up your kids. You feel like giving the principal a piece of your mind. What do you do?

Words to Lose	Words to Use
You act without thinking and jump in with both feet. *"Are you crazy? Why didn't you close the school in the first place?"*	You think before acting so your actions are wise, not rash. *"Let me put my mind in gear before I put my mouth in motion."*
You "go forth into battle" without considering the consequences. *"I just spent two hours in gridlock because of you. What a stupid decision. Didn't you check the weather?!"*	You talk yourself through the Choose Your Battles criteria. *"Let's see, what are the extenuating circumstances? I'm sure he made the best decision he could with the information he had at the time."*
You give this person a piece of your mind and tell him exactly how you feel. *"I'm going to call the board of supervisors and complain."*	You give yourself peace of mind by putting these circumstances in perspective. *"It must have been a damned-if-you-do, damned-if-you-don't decision."*

24

"Cats seem to go on the principle that it doesn't do any harm to ask for what you want."

—Joseph Wood Krutch

Use the Five Principles of Ethical Persuasion

Not only can it not hurt to ask for what we want, it can do a lot of harm to *not* ask for what we want. People can't read our minds. As discussed earlier, we can't wait for them to intuit how we feel and act on our behalf.

It is our responsibility to speak up for what we want, need, and deserve. Here's how you can do so ethically and persuasively.

Rule #1. Approach with positive expectations. You may think this is a blazing attack of the obvious. However, 'fess up—how many times have you approached people with a request while inwardly thinking, "This is a waste of time. They'll never agree to this." Winston Churchill said, "Before convincing others, we ourselves must be convinced." When we walk in with doubts, people sense them. If we don't believe our request is doable, why should they? Vow to walk in exuding conviction by repeating to yourself, "I know this will work. I'm sure this is a good idea [or fair request or worthwhile proposal]." Talk yourself into a state of assurance instead of talking yourself into a state of uncertainty.

Rule #2. Anticipate and voice their objections. It's imperative to put yourself in the "mind" of your decision maker(s) and figure out why they might say "no"—and then say it first. If you don't, they won't be listening to what you're saying. They'll be sitting there with their mental arms crossed waiting for you to stop talking so they can tell you why your idea won't work.

If you're proposing an expensive project and you predict they're thinking, "You've got to be crazy coming in and asking for this; we don't have money left in our budget," then guess what the first words out of your mouth better be?

"You may be wondering why I'm asking for money since we don't have any left in our budget." Then continue with, "*And*, if I can have your attention for the next five minutes, I'll explain how this project is going to save us that amount of money in the first sixty days." You have now defused their resistance.

Rule #3. Number and document each point. My high school speech teacher used to tell us, "Your expertise is judged by the organization of your thoughts." You may be the world's foremost authority on what you're presenting or proposing; however, if your thoughts are all over the map, your audience will conclude you don't know what you're talking about . . . even when you do.

Want to know the quickest way to aid comprehension and retention while lending legitimacy to your points? Number them. Enumerating your evidence organizes it and makes your line of reasoning sound objective rather than subjective. Listeners give numbered ideas more credence because they sound like facts, not opinions.

Furthermore, by saying, "There are three reasons this program is worth supporting. The first is . . . , the second is . . . , the third is . . ." listeners can more easily understand what you're saying because you're giving them a structure to follow. They'll be more persuaded because everything they're hearing "makes sense."

Rule #4: Meet *their* needs and speak *their* language. Remember this important point: people aren't motivated by *your* reasons—no matter how valid they are; they're motivated by how your idea will benefit *them*. Paul Harlan Collins offers a couple of marvelous one-liners that show this principle in practice: "The best way to get your teenager to shovel the driveway is to tell him he can use the car" and "If you want to teach your kids to count, give them different allowances."

Ask yourself, "What's important to the person I'm trying to persuade? Money? Status? Safety? Power? Advancement? How will my proposal be to their advantage?" If what's important to this person is her reputation as a respected visionary, then emphasize that she would be the first to implement this pioneering project and that her innovation would set the standard for years to come.

Rule #5: Motivate people to "try on" your ideas with real-life examples. People like to make up their own minds. Persuasion is not about peppering people with all the reasons why they should say yes. They'll often balk because they don't like being told what to do.

The key to effective persuasion is to use words like "imagine" and "picture" that cause people to *see* what we're saying so they're out of the passive, resistant state, and actively visualizing our proposal as if it were a done deal. Next, we want to use success stories that show how people *just like them* have already implemented these ideas to prove they work in real life, not just in theory.

Effective persuasion has both a left-brain, logical aspect and a right-brain, emotional aspect. Combine your factual, numbered points with human anecdotes and you'll increase the likelihood of people saying yes to your suggestion.

Appeal to the Head and to the Heart

"To know how to suggest is the great art of teaching."
—Ralph Waldo Emerson

A woman told me, "I volunteer in the career counseling center at my son's high school, and I am appalled at the students' behavior. When I went to school, kids had respect. These days, it seems like every other student uses the F word. When I walk down the halls, I hear students mouthing off to teachers; I see the older kids bullying the freshman. It's awful.

"I want to propose a character education program, but I'm afraid I'm going to get shot down. Some parents tried to put together a task force about this a few years ago, but it never got off the ground. Any suggestions?"

First, good for her for championing this worthwhile cause. Schools across the country that have instituted character education programs found they have made a positive difference. Here are some specific ways to incorporate the Five Principles of Persuasion so you can successfully pitch such a proposal.

Step #1. Instead of focusing on the fact that a similar proposal didn't get approved in the past, learn from and then avoid their mistakes. Remember what Dwight D. Eisenhower said, "Pessimism never won any battle." Talk yourself into a state of optimism so your enthusiasm sets the tone and becomes contagious. Tell yourself, "Character education programs are worthwhile, and I know everyone at our school will benefit from participating in them."

Step #2. Ask yourself why decision makers will say no. Do your homework and find out why people would not support this proposal. Perhaps some feel "values should be taught at home, not at school." Perhaps there's competition for funds and some people feel the money required for this program is better spent elsewhere. Once you identify the different forms of resistance, address them up front so listeners will give your ideas a chance.

Step #3. Formulate a certain number of points detailing the specific payoffs of your proposed plan. Visit www.CharacterCounts.com to research the tangible benefits that have occurred at schools that have sponsored these programs. If you are presenting your proposal in writing, generate as many different points as necessary to cover all the benefits; however, summarize them on *one page* so people can "eyeball" it and "get" the impact of the many advantages. If you deliver a fifty-page report, readers may be daunted by the sheer volume of material. They may scan it instead of read it and may miss some of your most important points.

If you are delivering your proposal in person, be sure to present no more than seven points. Seven is the number of items we can keep in short-term memory. (Think of our seven-digit phone numbers.) If you present more than seven points, the audience may feel overwhelmed and shut down; plus, they can't remember it all anyway. Feel free to back up your oral report with printed material outlining the other advantages, but discipline yourself to focus on the seven most important points.

Step #4. Avoid "I Statements." Engage with "You Questions." People won't be swayed by what *we* think and want. They will be swayed by a suggestion being presented so compellingly that they see how it will be in *their* best interests to act on it. See how weak it is to say, "*I* think this is a wonderful way to teach our kids respect." Change that into "Would you like to know how we could teach students to treat the faculty and each other with more respect?" Remember, declarative statements explaining what *we* think don't engage. Questioning (the Socratic method) is what involves listeners so they're considering our ideas instead of resisting them.

Next, identify the "pain" and the "problems" your proposal will fix. Ask teachers what they don't like. Ask students what bothers them about being at school. Ask parents what concerns them most about their children's behavior. Then, ask decision makers, "Would you like to know how to reduce fights, bullying, hate-crimes, and gang violence on campus? Would you like to know how to reduce vandalism and graffiti on school grounds? Would you like to know how to increase diversity-awareness and sensitivity? Would you like to know how to promote peaceful interactions and cooperation between staff and students?"

Then say, "If you will give me your attention for the next ten [fifteen?] minutes, you'll hear about a program that has done just that at hundreds of schools across the country and how it can accomplish that for our school too."

Step #5. Share success stories that turn this into a "want-to." In chapter 3, we talked about how people will do things willingly when they "want to," and reluctantly or not at all if they "have to." The beauty of using detailed anecdotes is they engage both the head (real-life examples are factual evidence) and the heart (true stories are emotionally appealing). Anecdotes will showcase how the program has already profited teachers, parents, students, staff, and administrators elsewhere. Upon hearing *substantiation* that this has already worked for others (in other words, this isn't speculative, it's proven), the school board becomes convinced and decides, "We want that for our school."

What If They Don't Approve Our Proposal?

"Never change a winning game, always change a losing one."
—Vince Lombardi

Are you thinking, "Well, this sounds good in theory. But what if I present my proposal for a character education program [or any proposal] and get turned down?" If that happens, don't give up. As Coach Lombardi said, we don't quit if our original tactics aren't victorious; we go back to the drawing board.

We can reopen "dead" issues if we unearth new evidence. Introducing a new point to the attention of decision makers, one not discussed in our initial negotiation, gives them justification for changing their minds and reaching a different conclusion. They can reverse themselves now without losing face because we have given them new criteria on which to base their decision.

So, if you get a no, use the Three Rs and Retreat, Reevaluate, and Reapproach.

Retreat

Exit the situation gracefully. If your proposal gets rejected, don't keep hammering on their door or you may find it slammed in your face. And don't slam the door on your way out, because you may want to walk back through it.

Reevaluate

Why did they turn you down? Did you not identify or meet their needs? Did you use "I statements" instead of "You questions"? Was your evidence underwhelming? Did you focus too much on facts and not enough on real-life stories they could relate to? Can you find new evidence proving the worthiness of this proposal that wasn't bought up the first time? Identify any weaknesses that may have sabotaged your success and strategize how you can strengthen your case.

Reapproach

Schedule a new hearing or appointment. Anticipate and neutralize their objections, i.e., "We've already turned this down" by prefacing your remarks with "I know we've discussed this before, and you might be interested in hearing about a recent study that casts new light on the situation." Then, present your ideas incorporating the Five Principles of Persuasion.

What is something you'd like to propose to your principal, school board, faculty, or teacher? If you want your request approved, it will be well worth the time and effort to study the Five Principles in advance. Figure out why they might say no, identify what's important to them, present numbered points, turn "I statements" into "You questions," and share a story that shows why your request is worth *their* while. It could be the difference between approval or dismissal.

Tongue Fu! Tip for Teens

Let me save you a lot of time. Whining doesn't work. If you want something, and want it bad, it's in your best interests to use these principles to ensure adults will listen.

My son Andrew is one of those kids who counted the days (hours?!) until he was old enough to get his driver's license. He also wanted his own car, and put together a compelling proposal for how to make that happen.

Step #1 Instead of filling his mind with doubts such as, "She'll never agree to this," he filled himself with convictions: "She'll agree to this as long as I cover all the bases."

Step #2 He anticipated my objections and neutralized them by saying, "I know you're wondering where the money is going to come from, and I've got it all worked out. I also know you're wondering whether I'm going to be responsible, and I'll show you how I am."

Step #3 He put together a five-point plan showing how he was going to 1) finance the car using money bequeathed to him by his grandfather, 2) be conservative by using only part of the money to buy a reliable, used car, 3) obtain the lowest insurance rates by keeping a good GPA so he got a "good student" discount, 4) help buy his own gas by getting a summer job as a lifeguard, and 5) take full financial responsibility for any damage caused by accidents.

Step #4 He met my needs by demonstrating how he was going to be financially responsible, and by addressing my major concern that he drive safely. He vowed to follow all rules (including a maximum of three passengers at a time), keep his car in good mechanical condition, and volunteered for his license be temporarily taken away if he received any tickets.

Step #5 He told the story of a friend, one I knew and respected, who had been driving since he was sixteen, and had designed and honored a similar arrangement.

Did Andrew get his car? Is this a rhetorical question? What wasn't to like? When an idea is presented this compellingly and comprehensively, it makes it comparatively easy to get a yes.

Action Plan for Use the Five Principles of Ethical Persuasion

You're the new football coach and you want the school to build a state-of-the-art weight room. You've coached champion teams before, and you think the difference between an average team and a winning team depends a lot on whether the players participate in a year-round strength-building program. What do you do?

Words to Lose	Words to Use
You talk yourself into a state of defeat.	You talk yourself into a state of determination.
"I don't even know why I'm wasting my time. They're going to turn me down flat."	*"I know this can make a big difference in the players' mental and physical development.*
You pitch your proposal without preparing.	You prepare your pitch with the Five Principles of Persuasion.
"So, this is what I want, and it'll only cost $150,000."	*"You might be thinking, 'Where are we going to find the money for this, and why should we?'"*

Words to Lose	Words to Use
You focus on what you think and want and are met with resistance. *"Our front liners average 180 pounds and that's just not big enough in this league."*	You focus on what they want and get their receptivity. *"You're probably concerned about risks and how we can make sure this equipment is used safely."*
You speak only from your experience and don't offer other evidence. *"Well, I've coached two other teams and it worked for them."*	You offer real-life examples that prove this has worked elsewhere. *"This article from Coach magazine reports a survey that says. . . ."*
You get a no and slam the door on your way out. *"You're going to be sorry when we embarrass ourselves and come in last in our league."*	You get a yes because they "want" what you've proposed. *"Thank you for approving this. You'll see the results on the playing field and in our win column."*

**"Why, since we are always complaining of our ills,
are we constantly employed in redoubling them?"**

—Voltaire

Hold People Accountable for Inappropriate Behavior

T oward the end of a Tongue Fu! workshop, a teacher raised her hand and said, "I agree with everything you're saying, and think these ideas work with most people most of the time. What if we're dealing with someone who ignores all this?"

Good question. I agree that these win–win Tongue Fu! techniques have the ability to motivate most people to respond *in kind*. It's true though, that a few people, for whatever reason, aren't motivated to cooperate.

With these people, whether young or old, it's important to draw the line and let them know they cannot get away with manipulative behavior. This chapter and the next share specific ideas on what to do if you've tried everything in your Tongue Fu! repertoire, and nothing's worked.

Name Their Game

"Don't fight forces, use them." —R. Buckminster Fuller

To paraphrase Fuller's quote, don't fight forces, name them. Naming someone's inappropriate behavior often has the power to neutralize it. A fundamental law of negotiation states: "A recognized tactic is no longer effective."

From now on, if someone is acting improperly, call them on it. How do you do this? Mentally step "outside" the situation and ask yourself, "What's happening here?" Then, *say it*. By doing so, you make the covert overt. By bringing their unhelpful conduct to the light of day, you can defuse it.

Want an example? Have you ever been the bearer of bad tidings? Did the recipient of the bad news dump their displeasure on you for reporting the unwelcome events, even though you didn't cause them?

This is what happened to one Gifted and Talented teacher who reported to a couple that their daughter hadn't scored high enough on the test to qualify for her class. "These two are the academic version of 'stage parents.' They're convinced their daughter is brilliant. She's certainly bright, however there are at least twenty other children who graded higher on the test than she did. They were relentless. They kept arguing with me even though this is a quantitative test that has measurable results.

"Do you know what finally got them off my case? I adopted the 'Why are you taking this out on me?' body posture by shrugging my shoulders, pointing my palms up toward the sky, and saying plaintively, 'Hey, don't kill the messenger.' It finally got through to them that this wasn't my fault, and they let up."

"Anger is momentary madness," observed the great poet Horace. Many people will stop making you the object of their anger if you "name their game" and make them aware of the fact that they're unloading on someone who's not responsible for what's bothering them. They'll often recant and say, "You're right, it's not fair to take this out on you. It's just that this is the last thing I needed to hear today."

A school secretary asked for help with a dilemma she was facing. "I work for the principal and the vice-principal, and they often give me conflicting work assignments. One will ask me to find the e-mail addresses of the school board, and then the other will drop a letter on my desk and ask me to proof it. One will give me a stack of paperwork to process, and the other will ask me to run off a flyer for the annual Sports Banquet. In the middle of all this, I'm also supposed to answer the phone and handle the front office. I don't know how much longer I can take this."

I told her to mentally step outside the situation so she could *see* it in perspective. "Now," I said, "Ask yourself, 'What's happening here?'" She thought about it for a minute and then brightened up when it occurred to her, "They're putting me in the middle!"

"Exactly," I said. "Next time they give you overlapping orders, don't suffer in silence or make best-guess decisions about which to tackle first. Say courteously, 'Please don't put me in the middle here. The principal has asked me to work on a different project and you're asking me to start on this. If you could please check with her as to which is the top priority, I'll be glad to get started on it.'"

What If Someone Is Swearing?

"Chaos, panic, disorder—my work here is done." —T-shirt slogan

Would you like to know what to do if people are causing panic and disorder by using abusive language?

Follow the advice of an experienced police officer who told me, "When we arrive on the scene of a fender bender, the drivers are usually distraught. Each has their own version of what happened and wants to get their side heard first. Emotions are high and tempers are short.

"I've found the best thing I can do to calm the chaos when people are at each other's throats is to take notes. First, I separate the two drivers, 'Ma'am, you stand over here. Sir, you stand over here.' I reassure them, 'Each of you will get your turn.' And then I pull out my notepad, turn to one of them, and say these magic words, 'Now, start at the beginning and tell me what happened.'"

He continued, "Nothing positive can be accomplished when people are shouting at each other. Asking them to chronicle what took place causes them to think back and reconstruct the chain of events. Now they're reporting instead of ranting and raving. This switches them from an emotional frame of mind to an objective frame of mind. Furthermore, they know I can't get everything down if they're talking a mile a minute, so they slow down. And when they slow down, they calm down.

"Have you ever noticed that when people are upset, they just keep repeating themselves? That's another reason taking notes works so well. About the third time they say something, I come back with, 'That's right, I've got that right here . . . and *then* what happened?' and it keeps them from rambling. After they've gotten everything off their chest, I read it back to them. Now they know their side of the story has been heard, and they're ready to move on."

Record Offensive Remarks

"Action is the antidote to despair." —Joan Baez

One teacher told me, "Documentation is essential these days. Not only does it convince people who are using abusive language to clean up their act, it is absolutely necessary to have written documentation of someone's over-the-line behavior for legal reasons. If I want to report someone's egregious behavior, or if I want to protect myself from someone who threatens to file a grievance against me, I need to have in writing exactly what was said, by whom, and when—and have that signed by witnesses if possible."

She continued, "I'm in charge of the dance team at our high school. A father stormed up to me after they performed during halftime at a home basketball game and said accusingly, 'Someone told me you're in charge of these girls. How can you let them wear these skimpy costumes and dance to that nasty rap music? That routine was downright pornographic,' and he continued to vent about how offended he was by them 'shaking their hips' . . . although he didn't say hips. The way I figured it, the man had a right to his opinion; however, he didn't have the right to call these young women names. I drew the line when he said, 'They should be ashamed of themselves for acting like w——!'

"I took out pen and paper from my backpack and said, 'Sir, could I please have your name and contact information so I can follow up on this? If you'd like to repeat what you just said, I'll make sure to get it down accurately.'

"As soon as I said that, he backed down. He was more than ready to lay his opinion on me; however, he wasn't so ready to be accountable for it. I still wrote down what he said and what I said and turned it into our vice principal, so if that parent followed up, the VP would have a record of what happened and could support my actions."

She's right. If, as Joan Baez pointed out, "Action is the antidote to despair," recording offensive remarks can be the antidote to disrespect.

Document Difficult Behavior

"Few are willing to brave the disapproval of their fellows, the censure of their colleagues, the wrath of their society. Moral courage is a rarer commodity than bravery in battle or great intelligence. Yet it is the one essential vital quality for those who seek to change the world." —Robert Kennedy

A friend who is a human resource director confirmed the importance of logging and reporting inappropriate behavior. She said, "If an employee complains to me about someone's unsuitable behavior, it's almost impossible for me to take action unless the date, time, and exact nature of the offending behavior have been documented. If you work with or around someone who is mistreating students or fellow faculty members, it's not enough to simply verbally report what happened. That's too subjective because it will end up being your word against theirs. If you want to change what's wrong, you must substantiate your claims by writing down *what* was said, *when*, and to *whom* so the decision maker has tangible evidence to investigate and act upon."

What If Someone Is Verbally Abusing Us on the Phone?

"Art, like morality, consists of drawing the line somewhere."
—G. K. Chesterton

A school counselor told me, "One of the most difficult aspects of my job is when I need to get involved with Child and Family Services on behalf of a student. If I suspect and/or have tangible evidence of domestic abuse and need to take action to remove a child from his or her home, the parent(s) are often volatile when I inform them of what's happening. It's a judgment call. There are times I'll decide to let a parent blow off steam if I think she or he's going to eventually calm down and we can discuss options and next steps.

"Other times, it's clear to me that this individual has no intention of calming down and is going to continue heaping abuse on me. If that's the case, I interrupt and say, 'Mr. [or Mrs.] _____, I want to help resolve this situation, and please speak to me with respect.' Even if they're screaming at me, I speak low and slow. By speaking in measured tones, I keep from adding emotional fuel to their fire.

"If they continue screaming or using foul language, I say one more time, 'Mr. [or Mrs.] _____, I will be glad to explain what's happening and why, and I'll ask one more time, please . . . speak . . . to . . . me . . . with . . . respect.' If they ignore that, I interrupt one last time and say, 'I am going to hang up now, and you are welcome to call back when you are ready to speak to me with respect.'

"As soon as I put the phone down, I immediately document the call so if she or he *does* call the principal and I get called into the office, I can supply my notes and say, 'That's right, Mr. ____ called at such and such time of day, this is what he said, and this is what I said,' so my principal can back me up.

"My goal is to show these parents that their verbal abuse will not be tolerated. I don't think we help matters by indulging adults when they throw temper tantrums. Someone has to say, 'This is not acceptable.' This out-of-control behavior is part of the reason Child and Family Services has been brought in, and we need to draw the line and say, 'You can't do this.'"

So, what are you going to do next time someone decides to make you the target of their verbal abuse? Do not silently endure the invective they hurl at you. Grab a notepad and paper and say, "Would you like to repeat that? I want to make sure I'm getting it down correctly," or interrupt them and quietly demand that they treat you with respect.

Tongue Fu! Tip for Teens

An unfortunate fact is that teenagers sometimes don't receive very courteous service at restaurants and retail establishments. My son triple-dated with several friends for his junior–senior prom and made reservations at a fancy waterfront restaurant. They got all dressed up, we proud parents recorded the Kodak moments with our cameras, and they loaded into a limo to head to the restaurant. They arrived for their 7:30 P.M. reservation and weren't seated until after 8 P.M. It took another half-hour to receive their menus. Tom's date went to the restroom and overheard their waiter talking to a bus boy. Their waiter was griping how "kids never leave big tips" and that he was going to "wait them out so they'll give up and leave."

She came back and told Tom. He got up from his seat, walked to the reception area and asked the hostess if he could please talk with the on-site manager. The manager came out and Tom politely explained the situation. The manager immediately apologized, said he would deal with the waiter later, told Tom he'd have someone else serve them immediately, offered them all complimentary desserts, and thanked Tom for bringing the matter to his attention,

If someone is mistreating you or verbally abusing you, don't retaliate. Either record their comments to motivate them to cease and desist, or ask firmly for them to treat you with respect. If they choose not to, document their behavior and/or politely report it to someone in power who has the authority to hold them accountable. Will this work every time? No. Will it work sometimes? Yes. Whatever happens, this course of action is better than yelling back or suffering in silence.

Action Plan for Hold People Accountable for Inappropriate Behavior

You are a counselor in charge of your school's peer mediation program. A parent storms into your office, upset because his son was found guilty of cheating and has been suspended from school for three days. The father is incensed that "a bunch of fifteen-year-olds" are disciplining his son. What do you do?

Words to Lose	Words to Use
You take umbrage.	You take notes.
"Hey, I don't like getting yelled at."	*"Sir, let me write this down."*

Words to Lose	Words to Use
You tell him to stop using foul language—and he continues using foul language. *"I don't get paid enough to listen to that kind of language. Cut out your swearing."*	You ask for his name and contact information so there'll be a record. *"Could I have your name and phone number so we can follow up on this?"*
You comment on his emotional behavior, which escalates it. *"You're blowing this all out of proportion and not making any sense."*	You move him into an objective frame of mind. *"Mr. Ross, please start at the beginning and tell me what. . . ."*
He keeps repeating himself because he feels you're not listening. *"How can you let kids make these kinds of decisions?! I'm outraged."*	You read back what he's said so he knows he's been heard. *"So, your son met with the peer mediation group on Wednesday, and. . . ."*

26

"The better we feel about ourselves, the fewer times we have to knock someone down to feel tall."

—Odetta

Break Free from Bullies

What if you try all these techniques and the person you're dealing with still continues to run roughshod over your rights? You're probably dealing with a bully, someone who knowingly and purposely takes advantage of others to get his or her way. Bullies don't want cooperation, they want control. They don't want a win-win, they want to win.

Idealistically, we would just avoid bullies and stay out of their path of wrath. Realistically, that's not always possible. If you work with, around, or for someone who seems to *delight* in making your life difficult, this chapter's for you.

Is Their Behavior a Onetime Thing or an Ongoing Habit?

"The tyrant crowds those he can't control, confuses those he can't convince, and crushes those he can't corrupt."
—Anonymous

I believe 90 to 95 percent of difficult behavior is situational. Someone is upset because something has gone wrong, and we happen to be the lightning rod for their anger. This type of person has "temporarily" lost his or her senses and is acting out of irritation. If we handle them sensitively and skillfully, we can often settle the issue and move forward.

The other 5 to 10 percent of difficult behavior is intentional. They are being ornery on purpose because 1) it gets the results they want, 2) they get some type of perverse thrill from it, and 3) they're not operating with a conscience. For this 5 to 10 percent, the end (getting their way) justifies the means—any means. They don't self-examine or self-correct. They don't respond to logic or reason because that doesn't matter to them. What matters to them is being on top, being the BMOC—Big Man (or Woman) on Campus—and being higher on the ladder. So, they knock people down and out of their way through belittling, undermining, name-calling, faultfinding, manipulation, domination, and histrionics.

How can you tell if someone is a bully—or just having a "bad day"? We all have "bad days." None of us are perfect. We all do or say things in the heat of the moment we wish we could take back. However, for the most part, those incidents are the exception, not the rule. The vast majority of people are accountable for their inappropriate behavior. We think, "Oh my gosh, I can't believe I said that!" The vast majority of us recognize when we've done something unfair and take steps to make amends.

Bullies don't. The following questions can help you determine if the person you're dealing with has the consistent *pattern* of characteristics that indicates whether they've crossed over into being a bully.

Bully for You? Questions

1. Do you have to "talk on eggshells" around this person and watch everything you say because she/he has a hair-trigger temper? Is she/he volatile and you never know when she's/he's going to blow up or why?
2. Does this person make disparaging remarks, and then turn around and accuse you of being "too sensitive" if you take offense? Does she/he taunt you and then claim she/he was "Just kidding?" Does she/he turn on anyone who "dares" to question his judgment, authority, or "rightness"?
3. Is she/he bitter and holds a lot of animosity toward others? Does she/he frequently find fault with others and/or blame

everyone else for what goes wrong? Does she/he get dispropor-
tionately upset if you ever try to point out how she/he could
have played a role in how events unfolded?

4. Does this person crowd you by getting too close; use a snide,
sarcastic, or loud voice to intimidate you; or invade your physical space with inappropriate touching or physical violence?

5. Does this person play "martyr"? Does she/he try to make everyone else feel sorry for her/his unhappiness? Does she/he hold
others responsible for her/his problems or lack of success?

6. Does this person purposely humiliate people to show off
her/his power and prove her/his superiority? Does she/he pick
fights in public because she/he knows people won't fight back
because they don't want to make a scene?

7. Is this person dissonant? Is she/he a two-faced, Jekyll-Hyde
character—capable of charm one minute (when it suits her/his
purposes) and cruelty the next?

8. Does this person deliberately pinpoint and pick on other people's weakness to control them and make them feel ashamed?
Does this person use cunning or cruelty to "target" and "eliminate" people who are in her/his way?

9. Does this person keep people off balance by twisting their
words? Does she/he engage in crazy-making behavior—making
and then breaking promises and then claiming to never have
made them in the first place, etc.

10. Do you often catch this person in a lie? Does she/he play fast
and loose with the truth? Does she/he exaggerate her/his
achievements, claim to have done things she/he never did, and
seem to have no remorse or conscience for being dishonest?

11. Is this person a covert (not overt) manipulator? Is it hard to put
your finger on exactly what this person does—all you know is
she/he makes you feel slimed, used, or lesser-than? Does she/he
engage in sly, passive-aggressive behavior?

Stop Bullies from Using You as Target Practice

"You have got to have courage. I don't care how good a man is, if
he is timid, his value is limited. I want to see a good man able to
hold his own against the force of evil." —Theodore Roosevelt

If the person you're dealing with *regularly* engages in six or more of the above behaviors, or if you've already tried everything in your win–win repertoire to resolve things amicably with this individual—to no avail—you're probably dealing with a bully. It's time to step up your response. It's time to "Do the You."

Most of us have been taught to use the word *I* when expressing our dissatisfaction with how someone's treating us. We're supposed to say, "*I* don't like it when you accuse me of not caring about my students" or "*I* feel hurt when you say I'm not doing a good job teaching your daughter." By expressing our opinions with the *I* word, we are owning our emotions instead of blaming other people for how we feel.

That's a mature and healthy way to interact—and as long as both people take responsibility for doing this, it is the best way to move through differences to an amicable resolution.

Unfortunately, *I* statements backfire with bullies. Remember, bullies don't "own" their behavior. Using "I" statements with a bully sets up double jeopardy because it becomes *our* fault that we don't like being mistreated. If we say, "I don't like being chastised in front of my students" they'll say, "Well, then you should do a better job keeping them under control." If we say, "I don't like being called names," they'll say "Grow up" or "Get used to it." *I* statements keep the attention on *our* reaction and make us seem like we're oversensitive "cry-babies."

Furthermore, bullies *want* us to be upset by their remarks. When we talk about how hurt we feel, they don't feel remorse, they feel victorious because they know their taunts are working. *I* statements actually reward bullies because they prove that the bully is "getting to us." It perpetuates their power trip.

That's why, from now on, if you have determined that this person is a bully, use the word "you" instead of the word "I." Yes, this flies in the face of what you've been told. However, it works with people who have ignored all your fair-minded attempts to get along, because it keeps the attention where it belongs—on *their* inappropriate behavior. The following is an example.

Don't Let Bullies Get Away with Their Behavior

"What we accept, we teach." —poster in Child and Family
Services office

A friend's daughter role-modeled how we can use the word "you" to stop bullies from verbally victimizing us. This young woman was graduating from Georgetown University on the same day her younger sister was graduating from a high school on Maui. Her mother, who was still recovering from a bitter divorce, couldn't be in two places at once and had elected to stay in Hawaii. Unbeknownst to any of them, the girls' father, who was "persona non grata" at the time, found out about the Georgetown graduation and showed up, unannounced and uninvited.

No sooner had the daughter received her diploma then her father approached and started in with his normal-for-him hypercritical comments: "You just wasted four years of your life. Why'd you get a degree in political science, anyway? You're never going to be able to find a job. You just threw away thousands of dollars."

He would have continued his verbal assault, but the self-assured young woman put her hand up and startled her father into silence. She looked him in the eye and said slowly and purposefully, "Dad, stop. *Do I look like my mother?*"

He stared at her in shock, mouth hanging open. She continued, "I am proud of myself for graduating from this university, and I'm glad I got this degree. If you are here to help me celebrate, you're welcome to stay. If you're not, leave."

Bravo. *That* is how to deal with a bully. Notice, she didn't lose her temper and start calling him names. She didn't wilt under his criticism and suffer in silence, only to go home later that night devastated because he had ruined her big day. Nor did she break into tears and use *I* words to express how hurt she was by this undeserved attack.

She held up her hand to stop him midsentence. She didn't tell him how hurt she "felt" about his ridicule, she used the word "you" to keep the focus on his inappropriate behavior and to let him know in no uncertain terms that it would not be tolerated.

Don't Tiptoe around a Bully

"If you put a small value on yourself, rest assured that the world will not raise your price." —Anonymous

Bullies push, push, push as a way of taking our measure. In a perverse way, they only respect the people who say, "You're not getting away with that here." To a bully, silence means acceptance. If we "turn the other cheek" or back down (because we're trying to avoid a confrontation or keep the peace) we perpetuate the bully's behavior because they know they can have their way with us.

Appealing to a bully's good nature rarely works; she/he may not have one. Although it runs contrary to how we want to be with most people, a good offense can be the best defense when dealing with abusive personalities. I will always remember a silver-haired, mild-mannered woman who sat in the back row of one of my public seminars. When I was sharing these rather radical suggestions, she nodded along in agreement. She finally put her hand up and said, "I've been a school counselor for more than thirty years. What I've learned is sometimes you've got to 'bully the bully.' Bullies see everyone on a ladder—you're either lower on the ladder or higher. We'd love to believe that children are perfect little angels; however, school is one big pecking order. They're constantly trying to establish who's Queen Bee and who's Top Dog. When you let them know up front that you won't allow that kind of behavior, you establish yourself as the 'Alpha' and they stop testing you."

She said, "Please don't misunderstand me. I absolutely believe in finding and nurturing the good in each child. I love working with children and I do my best to be a positive influence in their lives. I just think I'm doing them—and me—a favor by not tolerating any bullying to or around me."

Do the You

"There are no victims without volunteers." —anonymous

From now on, if you have taken the AAA Train, taken notes, taken on the person's point of view by reflecting on what they're saying, and tried everything you can think of to resolve the situation—and nothing's worked—it's time to "Do the You." Don't wait for them to stop talking. Interrupt their inappropriate behavior and say:

- "Change your language. That is unacceptable."
- "Back off and keep your hands to yourself."
- "You. Sit down and make silence."
- "Enough. Keep those kinds of comments to yourself."

- "Wait a minute. You don't want a written record of those remarks."
- "Stop right there. That's out of line and you know it."
- "You need to lower your voice and speak to me with respect."
- "Nobody talks to me that way. Try again, without the name-calling."
- "You either speak to me with respect or this conversation is over."
- "You used to get away with that; you don't get away with that anymore."
- "Think again. Guilt trips don't work with me."
- "You might want to rephrase that. It doesn't reflect well on you."
- "Do other people actually let you get away with that?! Not here!"
- "You've crossed the line. That was inappropriate and you know it."

A junior high coach told me he "did the you" with his basketball team. The first day of practice, he handed out uniforms to the players. In addition to the official game uniforms, they had team T-shirts with the school's logo on them for practice. The gym was often overheated in wintertime, and with all the drills and running up and down the court, the players were often covered with sweat halfway through the practice. The coach told the team it was okay to cut off the sleeves of their T-shirts so they wouldn't get overheated. The next day, a player ran up to him, his T-shirt sopping wet and said, "Looks like I need another '*wife-beater*'" (an offensive, slang term for T-shirts with the arms cut off).

The coach looked at him in shock and said, "*What did you just say*?!" The kid repeated, "You know, these wife-beater T-shirts. I need another one." The coach said, "That term is offensive. Pick another word to call those shirts." The player said, "Okay" and that was the end of that.

If the coach hadn't said anything, the player would have thought nothing of continuing to use that term. Next time someone says something offensive to you, don't look the other way and don't turn the other cheek. Do the you.

Stand Up and Stand Strong

"What we accept, we teach." —Anonymous

Why do people become bullies? Well, that's a whole book in itself. In fact, in addition to my book on this topic, *Take the Bully by the Horns*, I'd like to recommend Barbara Coloroso's (author of *Kids Are Worth It!*)

new book *The Bully, the Bullied, and the Bystander*. It's packed with specific suggestions on what to do when people consistently step over the line of common decency and "how parents and teachers can help break the cycle of violence."

It has been a challenge trying to condense all the important information about bullies into this one chapter, because there are many reasons people become bullies, and many strategies on how to deal with different types of bullies. Suffice it to say, I only have space to share a couple of the ideas that educators and students can use to deal more effectively with bullies at school.

If you have bullies in your life, it is in your best interest to read *Take the Bully by the Horns*. I'm partial of course; it's just that many people have told me it's an eye-opener because I don't paint a rosy scene of how we can turn bullies around by simply being kinder to them. I wish that were true; however, the truth is most bullies don't respect or respond to kindness, they take advantage of it. That book has dozens of ways you can continue to act with integrity, and yet not allow a bully to run rampant over you.

Is Their Behavior Dangerous?

> "Fear is a kind of bell or gong which rings the mind into quick life
> on the approach of danger. It is the soul's signal for rallying."
> —Henry Ward Beecher

In today's violent world of metal detectors at schools, knives and guns in lockers, gang fights, substance abusers under the influence, and threats of bodily harm, it's important not to take risks that could put us in danger.

If you're dealing with someone who you sense could erupt into violence, it's best to remove yourself and others from the scene and contact security officers who are trained to deal with this level of physical aggression. If someone has dilated pupils, a vacant stare, wild and rolling eyes, slurred or nonsensical speech, and/or clumsy, unbalanced movement, it's best not to confront them. They may be in an altered state where they are not acting reasonably, and they're a danger to themselves and others.

Marine General P. O. Smith once said, "We're not retreating. We're just advancing in the opposite direction!" If your instincts tell you the person you're dealing with is dangerous, head the opposite direction. Put your personal safety, rather than your pride, first. I'm not suggesting you turn a blind eye to hazardous behavior. I'm suggesting you think first before confronting someone who could put you in the hospital (or worse). As my friend Judy says, "Better smart than sorry."

Tongue Fu! Tip for Teens

A vanload of teenage boys told me: "Mrs. Horn, the advice adults give us about bullies is a joke. They tell us, 'If someone picks on you, just walk away.' Right!" they snorted. "If we walk away, the bully will come after us. Parents tell us, 'Bullies are just looking for attention. Ignore them and they'll leave you alone.'" They all snorted again. "Who likes to be ignored? They'll just get in our face so we're forced to pay attention to them. Parents tell us to tell a teacher if someone's picking on us. Teachers just tell us 'I didn't see it, so I can't do anything about it.' Or, if the bullies do get in trouble, they get suspended, which is what most of them want anyway."

A 2000 study by the National Association of School Psychologists reported that more than 160,000 children a day skip school because they fear a bully. This is an everyday threat that almost every school-aged child in our country faces Monday through Friday.

Are you thinking, "Tell me something I don't know"? The question, of course, is what can we do about it. Some schools have instituted character education and violence prevention programs, and that can help. Some schools have instituted peer mediation boards and zero tolerance, and that has helped. It still comes down to what can you do as an individual when kids are on your case. The answer may surprise you.

Do you have a cat and dog at home? Who rules the roost? Have you ever noticed how your cat usually is in charge, even if your dog is three times its size? Look at what happens when your dog gets near your cat. Your cat probably arches her back, puffs up, and glowers at your dog with a "Don't even think about it" look. Your dog probably backs off and gives your cat a wide berth. Maybe your dog and cat get along great. If they do, it's probably because the cat asserted her boundaries in the beginning and the dog now respects them and doesn't get too rough.

I see this phenomenon played out every time I take our Jack Russell out for a walk. We have a calico cat in our neighborhood who turns tail and runs every time she sees us coming. Our dog Murph is at the end of her leash straining to go after that cat.

On the other hand, there's Mr. Gray Cat. Mr. Gray Cat doesn't run from anybody, no matter how big. When Mr. Gray Cat sees us, there's no other word for it—he expands. He draws himself up to his full height, narrows his eyes, and glares at Murph. Murph won't get near that cat. Now, the fact of the matter is, most dogs would win a battle with a cat if they tried, but they don't try if the cat holds its ground.

Be a Cool Cat, Not a Scaredy Cat

"It's not the size of the dog in the fight, it's the size of the fight in the dog." —Dwight Eisenhower

When it comes to dealing with bullies, I think we need to be more like a "cool cat" and less like a "scaredy cat." Bullies operate at a more animalistic level rather than humanistic level. They sense and seek fear. If they see someone avoiding, cowering, or retreating, it *invites* their "chase instinct."

See, bullies operate on a risk–reward ratio. They don't pick on people who look like they're going to give them a hard time. They don't want to risk getting shown up. They pick on the easy targets—the calico cats—the meek ones who try to slink away. They leave the strong ones alone.

So, what's this mean for you? *I am not suggesting we fight.* In the aftermath of the tragic events at Columbine and other schools that have experienced violent acts of retaliation, fighting is not an option. I am suggesting you tower instead of cower. I am suggesting you stand tall instead of hunch over. I am suggesting you hold your chin up instead of duck it down and avoid eye contact. By projecting an "I'm comfortable with myself" attitude instead of a pleading "Don't hurt me" attitude, bullies will tend to walk on by.

Tower Instead of Cower

"I went to a really tough school. We wrote essays on what we wanted to be if we grew up." —Lenny Bruce

I had an opportunity to be on the TV show *To Tell the Truth*. While in "make-up" getting readied for my appearance as "Will the real Sam Horn, author of Tongue Fu! please stand up?" I noticed a picture of the make-up artist with his young son, both outfitted in karate attire, receiving trophies. I asked about it and he explained, "My son was always the smallest kid in his class and he always got picked on. He was miserable. He's a really nice kid and he never wanted to fight, but they just wouldn't leave him alone.

"I decided I had to do something about it, so I enrolled both of us in a martial arts class. The very first night, the instructor walked up to my son, gently pushed a finger in my son's chest, and knocked him off balance. He was pointing out that most of us are 'easy to push around.' We're not grounded in our strength—we're 'pushovers.'

"He then taught us how to move our mind down into our gut and root ourselves down through our legs into the ground so we are more centered. It was amazing. A few minutes later, he walked up to my son, placed his finger on his chest and pushed. This time my son stood his ground and absorbed the push without getting knocked off balance.

"My son has never had to use his martial arts skills to defend himself, and that wasn't really the point anyway. The point is, he carries himself differently. He walks with his head up and projects a natural confidence that doesn't invite predators. One time at school, they were in gym and a boy who had bullied him before bounced a basketball off his head. Instead of pretending it didn't bother him (which would have empowered the bully) he looked him in the eye and said, 'Do you feel better about yourself now? Is that what you have to do to feel good about yourself?' He didn't wimp out, he just turned the tables on the bully. He's still the smallest kid in the class. It's just that he's so comfortable with himself now, the bullies leave him alone. It's wonderful to see."

In the next chapter, we'll talk about more ways to act confident—even if you don't feel confident. Because—as Mr. Gray Cat and Mr. Calico Cat demonstrate—how confident we are has a lot to do with whether bullies come after us or choose to leave us alone.

Action Plan for Break Free from Bullies

You're patrolling the playground during recess and notice two kids getting into it. You head over to intervene. What do you do?

Words to Lose	Words to Use
You appeal to their "reason," not noticing whether they have a pattern of bully behavior. *"Is it nice to hit other children? Would you like it if someone did that to you?"*	You know these two have a history of aggression, so you intervene with strength. *"You two back off and give each other space, now!"*
You start off with 'I' words, and they ignore you. *"I don't like to see you fighting."*	You use the word "you" to keep the attention on their behavior. *"You need to clean up your language, now. Don't even think about using that word around me!"*
You say how you feel about their behavior and they keep at each other. *"I get upset when I see children hitting each other. It's just not right."*	You ask for their names and pull out a notepad so they know there'll be a record of their remarks. *"Next word out of your mouth gets written down and reported."*
You meekly ask for their cooperation and they feel you're weak. *"Now, I want you two to get along from now on, okay?"*	You tell them what's expected and make clear you're in charge. *"You two will stay ten feet away from each other. Show me what ten feet looks like, now."*

PART IV

Manage Your Emotions vs. Letting Them Manage You

"Life appears to me too short to be spent in nursing animosity or registering wrongs."

—CHARLOTTE BRONTË

27

"I was always looking outside myself for strength and confidence, but it comes from within. It is there all the time."

—Anna Freud

Act Confident Even When You Don't Feel Confident

A teacher told me, "I agree that confidence plays a big role in whether people treat us with respect. The question is, how can we act confident if we don't feel confident?"

Want good news? There is a direct and dramatic way to boost your confidence. It's based on an important discovery regarding the link between emotions and actions. William James, a respected human behavioral psychologist said this was one of the most important insights he learned in his forty-plus years of studying human behavior.

James observed that feeling *follows* action, not the other way around.

Many of us believe that feeling *produces* action. In other words, we feel afraid, so we act afraid. The opposite is true. Our timid behavior is the cause of our fear, not the result. If we want to feel more confident, the most direct and dramatic way to achieve that is to adopt an "aura of authority"—a body posture that says "I'm in charge of myself and comfortable in my own skin."

Put up a Brave Front

"I pretended to be somebody I wanted to be until finally I became that person. Or he became me." —Cary Grant

From now on, instead of letting your body *reflect* how you feel, make your body *direct* how you feel. If you wait until you feel self-assured to act self-assured, you could be waiting a long time. Starting today, stand strong so you feel strong. How do you do that?

Are you near a mirror right now? Take a minute to walk over and look at yourself. Let your shoulders droop and your chest cave in. Stand slouched, with your feet and knees close together. Duck your head, tuck in your chin, and look out and up at the world with tentative eyes. Now, assume the fig leaf position. Yup, cup your hands in front of you, or clasp your arms together.

Do you feel hesitant and insecure? This "cower" posture not only looks weak and submissive to other people, but it also causes you to feel anxious and unsure of yourself. Criminals and bullies actually look for this "victim" stance because it makes a person look like an easy target.

Now, stand up straight and square your shoulders. Hold your chin up and look at the "world" with a level gaze. Stand with your feet shoulder-width apart—the balanced athlete's stance. Move your hands away from the protective posture and hold them naturally at your sides. This "tower" posture says to the world, "I know who I am." People will regard you with more respect because you obviously hold yourself in respect. Aggressors looking to prove themselves will take one look at your confident body language and think, "I'm not going to mess with this person. She can take care of herself."

Overcome Learned Helplessness

"Bullies are always to be found where there are cowards."
—Mahatma Gandhi

A teacher told me, "Posture is not petty. I put my female students in front of a mirror and show them what it looks like to 'simper.' When they curve their shoulders in, and put on this cajoling expression, it makes them look subservient. It's one thing to flirt, it's another to permanently walk and talk with a docile, deferential body language that fairly shouts out, 'I'm the weaker sex.'

"I also recommend that they wear a backpack instead of hold their schoolbooks in front of them. Hugging their books to their chest rolls their shoulders forward and makes them look hunched over and vulnerable. Wearing a backpack helps free up their arms so they can walk tall with strong, purposeful strides instead of meek little steps. It really makes a difference in how they're perceived and treated."

She continued, "Standing and walking differently is one way to help them act and feel more confident. I've got a couple of girls in my class, though, who are easily intimidated. It's like they're scared of their own shadow. Isn't there something else I can do to help them become more sure of themselves?"

Yes, there is. First, it's important to understand that when we lack confidence, it's often a result of "learned helplessness." This is a dispirited mental state that results from being repeatedly put in situations in which we feel powerless. Anxiety is defined as "not knowing." If we "don't know" what to say or do when someone challenges us, we don't handle ourselves well in that situation, which makes us even more afraid of that person and more fearful of that situation. Our discomfort manifests itself in apprehension, which is perceived by aggressors. The aggressors then take advantage of our awkwardness, which causes us to feel even more intimidated, and down, down, the spiral we go.

The way to counteract learned helplessness is to practice putting ourselves in situations that petrify us—and practice responding with power and poise instead of panic. Anxiety is feeling "I can't." Confidence is feeling "I can." By repeatedly rehearsing formerly intimidating scenarios and now acting with assurance rather than apprehension, we train ourselves to comfortably handle those situations. We are tuning anxiety (not knowing what to do and say) into confidence (knowing what to do and say.)

Don't Worry, Rehearse

"Strength is a matter of the made-up mind." —John Beecher

Confidence is a result of a well-rehearsed mind. Please think of an event coming up that's making your knees knock and your palms sweat.

Will you be presenting your budget requests to a school board? Are you going to be meeting with parents who are angry because they've just learned their son failed two courses and won't be graduating with his class? Do you need to counsel a faculty member who has not been performing to standard?

Would you like to walk into that situation with poise rather than panic? Then vow to spend your time before that event mentally rehearsing instead of worrying. It's been said that visualizing—mentally rehearsing—is the single best thing we can do to produce confident performance. That is a rather grandiose claim. Why is mental rehearsal so powerful?

1. **Confidence is based on recent, frequent, successful practice.** Think about it. If we do something well, we do it a lot, and we've done it recently, we can walk into a situation with confidence. Confidence can be defined in one word as "trust." We trust that we can perform well in a situation when we have done well many times before.

2. **Nervousness is caused by focusing on our doubts and fears.** If we're thinking, "What if I make a fool of myself in front of the board?" "What if I get brain-freeze and forget what I was going to say?" we will talk ourselves into a state of dread. Nervousness is simply the result of concentrating on worst-case scenarios.

3. **We are uncomfortable in unfamiliar situations.** In new surroundings, our system produces adrenaline so we will be prepared to escape or defend ourselves if necessary. This instinctive "flight or fight" mechanism kicks in whenever we encounter the unknown, because we don't know what to expect. Only after we've spent time in a place and know it's safe can we relax and release the nervous energy that accompanies untested waters.

4. **Our mind doesn't differentiate between what's real and what's imagined.** This isn't pop psychology. If we vividly imagine or remember something happening, our mind and body "experience" it is as if it were actually happening. For example, just thinking about a near car accident we had this morning can bring back the same surge of panic we felt when that car came out of nowhere and almost sideswiped us.

5. **Practice makes better, and planned, precise practice makes even better.** The way we acquire abilities (whether it's driving a car or speaking confidently in front of a group) is to identify

the fundamentals and run through them again and again until we can do them flawlessly.

Let's put all that together and see what we've got. Mentally rehearsing *what* we want to say and *how* we want to act:

- Gives us recent, frequent, successful practice that gives us confidence. We trust we'll be able to perform well because we've already done so.
- Reduces nervousness because we're not thinking about our doubts and fears; we're filling our mind with best-case scenarios.
- Repeatedly puts us in the situation we're about to encounter, which means we can walk in with confidence because we've "been there, done that."
- Increases the likelihood that we'll perform confidently in the "real" situation because we've been practicing confident performance— and our mind doesn't register or care that this wasn't "actual" practice.
- Accelerates our improvement. Real-life practice is beneficial; however, we can't do it perfectly every time, so we're actually imprinting mistakes. Precise, planned, positive mental practice expedites our ability to act confidently because in our minds, we're doing it right every time.

Turn Your Doubts into Determination

"Doubt is a pain too lonely to know that faith is his brother."
—Kahlil Gibran

A student told me, "I've been selected as valedictorian. I've never spoken to a group of more than thirty people, and there will probably be two thousand people there that day. I can't sleep at night; I can't keep my mind on my studies. All I can think about is getting up there and blowing it in front of two thousand people."

I asked Melodie, "How long do you have before graduation?"

She said, "Two weeks."

I replied, "You can spend the next two weeks worrying, or you can spend the next two weeks rehearsing. Which is a better use of your thought time?"

She smiled and said, "Rehearsing. But how do I rehearse so I can get up there and not be afraid?" I suggested she follow these steps.

1. **Duplicate the real-life situation as closely as possible in your mind.** I asked, "Where will graduation be held?" She told me, "In our gym." I asked, "Where will you be seated? Who will introduce you?" I suggested she fill in as many details as possible so she could vividly imagine herself speaking to that crowd *in that space* whenever she practiced. The more detailed she is in picturing what it will be like that day, the more she "puts herself there" in her mind, and the more comfortable she'll be when the day comes because she'll have "been there, done that."

2. **Rehearse your presentation precisely, word for word with full expression, from beginning to end.** Mental practice is ineffective if you jump around from scene to scene or if you give a halfhearted, distracted effort. Pop Warner said, "We play the way we practice." If we practice lazily, we'll perform lazily. We can't give 50 percent effort and expect to magically get up and be our 100 percent best. Mentally rehearse as if you were in front of the group, giving your best talk.

3. **Play devil's advocate. Imagine your worst-case scenario and plan how you can prevent it or rebound if it happens.** Melodie looked at me like I was crazy. "Aren't you contradicting yourself? I thought you told us focusing on our fears would make us nervous." "You're right," I replied. "The idea isn't to dwell on our fears to become more apprehensive, the idea is to anticipate what could go wrong and prepare for it." By strategizing in advance, we can avoid negative situations or turn them into an advantage by handling them well.

    I asked, "What are you most afraid of?" "That my mind will go blank." "Okay then, practice losing your train of thought." "What?!" she squawked. "Break your presentation into three or four segments," I replied, "and assign them a lead-in line that you get to know so well, you can say it in your sleep. If you forget where you are, just say, 'Which brings me to my next point' and continue."

4. **Finally, repeatedly run through your desired vs. dreaded performance.** As discussed earlier, the mind can't focus on the opposite of an instruction. I asked Melodie, "If you tell yourself, 'I don't have anything to be afraid of' or 'I hope I don't forget what I'm

going to say' what will happen? Fill your mind with what you *want* to happen so it imprints and produces that. Say to yourself, 'I'm looking forward to this. What an opportunity and a privilege. I am so proud and grateful to share this message with this group. I will remember my four points and present them eloquently and persuasively. I am going to enjoy and revel in every moment.' "

See Speaking As an Opportunity, Not an Onerous Obligation

"Mend your speech a little lest you mar your fortunes."
—Shakespeare

Melodie called me after her graduation to report in, "It went wonderfully. I was so relaxed up there. I felt like I'd done it a hundred times before!" She *had* done it a hundred times before—in the comfort of her own home. Thanks to her mental rehearsal, she was able to deliver her message with confidence.

It's presumptuous to think I could improve on Shakespeare, but wouldn't you agree we should mend our speech so we can *make* our fortunes? The ability to get our points across confidently and effectively is one of the most important personal and professional skills we can have. It's as important as talent and intelligence. We can be brilliant, but if we can't express ourselves in a way that gains interest and respect, we've neutralized our effectiveness. We may want to coexist cooperatively, but if we can't communicate constructively, we will sabotage our efforts to get along.

Power is defined as "the ability to get things done." Our ability to get things done depends on our ability to educate and motivate through words. Simply said, if we want to increase our effectiveness, we need to communicate effectively, and if we want to improve our ability to communicate effectively, we need to mentally rehearse so we can say *what* we want, *when* we want, the *way* we want, to *whom* we want.

Does visualization guarantee success? Of course not. It does guarantee progress. Our real-life event won't go as "scripted"; however, it will certainly go more smoothly than if we walk in cold. We may not be "perfect"; however, we will be more confident than if we had concentrated solely on our concerns. And, we will be taking responsibility for forging our fate instead of allowing ourselves to become passive victims of fate.

Tongue Fu! Tip for Teens

You may have heard or read somewhere that James Earl Jones—he of the booming, deep bass voice of Darth Vader in the *Star Wars* trilogy—stuttered as a child. He describes his growing up years as being wretched because his peers taunted him mercilessly about his inability to speak. Fortunately, he was blessed with a speech therapist in high school who taught him how to enunciate clearly and speak confidently—and his life was altered forever because of that intervention.

It's hard to overstate the importance of being able to communicate confidently. You may be thinking, "Well, you make your living from speaking, so you're biased about this." You're right. I am biased, because I've had the privilege of leading a blessed life due to my ability to get up in front of a group of people and share messages that are meaningful to me, and that make a difference for them.

It doesn't matter *what* you want to do with your life. It doesn't matter if you have no idea what profession you want to pursue or what field you want to study. Signing up for a speech class at your high school, joining the debate team, entering speech competitions, or participating in Toastmasters (an international group that teaches how to speak publicly) could be the single best investment you make in your future.

Whether it's fair or not, discomfort, uneasiness, or embarrassment about speaking compromises our effectiveness. People think less of us. We may not score well on an oral interview even though we know our stuff. We may not get hired for a job even though we're qualified. Mentally rehearse before presenting your ideas so you can speak with confidence. Invest time in developing your ability to say what you mean—it will serve you all your days.

Action Plan for Act Confident Even When You Don't Feel Confident

You have been nominated for Teacher of the Year for your county. You're proud to have been honored for your work; however, you just found out two of the judges will be coming to your classroom next week to observe you in action, and you're nervous about their visit. What do you do?

Words to Lose	Words to Use
You talk yourself into a state of dread. *"What if the kids act up while the judge is there?"*	You talk yourself into a state of determination. *"We will practice how to behave during the judge's visit."*
You focus on your doubts and fears and become more nervous. *"I've only been a teacher five years. I'm probably competing with teachers who have been doing this for twenty years."*	You mentally rehearse how you're going to stay calm and collected. *"I'm honored to have my work recognized and I can't wait to show what we're doing in class."*
You worry about what could go wrong and dwell on worst-case scenarios. *"I would be so humiliated if our science experiment didn't work or if the students weren't able to answer her questions."*	You prepare for what could go wrong, and then run through and imprint best-case scenarios. *"If the science experiment doesn't work, we'll talk about what we learned, and then we'll brainstorm possible solutions."*

28

"We cannot cure the world of sorrow, but we can choose to live in joy."

—Joseph Campbell

Maintain a Positive Perspective

A professor named Martha told me, "I don't have a problem with confidence. What I need help with is, well, for lack of a better phrase, my smoldering resentment. The head of our department and I don't get along—to say the least. I have no respect for the woman and she seems to go out of her way to give me grief. I've thought about quitting, but there's no way I'm going to give up my tenure and start at the bottom again somewhere else. There are days I go home with smoke coming out of my ears because of something she's done. Help?"

I was glad Martha asked this because it gave me an opportunity to share one of the most popular Tongue Fu! stories. Toward the end of a public seminar, I put a transparency with Eleanor Roosevelt's famous quote up on the overhead. The original quote is, "*No one can make us feel inferior without our consent*," and I had modified it to say, "*No one can make us angry or depressed without our consent.*"

A gruff construction boss raised his hand and said, "Sam, you're pulling a Pollyanna with this one. You have no idea the kind of people I work with. Do you mean if someone is swearing at me, I'm not supposed to get mad?"

Unclench Your Mind

"No man can think clearly when his fists are clenched."
—George Jean Nathan

A woman in the audience stood up and said, "I agree with this because I've lived through it. I'm a surgical nurse. I work with a neurosurgeon who is the most abrasive individual I've ever worked with. He is a brilliant physician, but he's got zip people skills. Last year, I was a fraction of a second late handing him an instrument in surgery. He berated me in front of my peers. He humiliated me in front of the medical staff. It took all my professionalism just to finish the operation and not walk out.

"Later, while driving home, I started thinking about what he had said to me. I got so upset. I got home, sat down at the dinner table, and told my husband what had happened. I clenched my fists and said, '*That doctor makes me so mad.*'"

"My husband had heard this before. He looked at me calmly and asked, 'Judy, what time is it?'

"Puzzled, I looked at him and said, 'Seven o'clock.'

"'What time did this happen?'

"'Nine o'clock this morning.'

"'Judy,' he asked, 'Is it the doctor who's making you mad?' And with that, he got up and left the table.

"I sat there and thought about it, and realized it wasn't the doctor who was making me mad. The doctor wasn't even in the room. I was the one who had given him a ride home in my car. I was the one who set him a place at my dinner table. I decided that evening that never again was that doctor welcome in my home or in my head. When I left the hospital, he was staying there and never again was I going to give him the power to poison my personal life."

Who's Making You Mad?

"Not to have control over the senses is like sailing in a rudderless ship, bound to break to pieces upon coming into contact with the very first rock." —Mahatma Gandhi

Who do you bring home with you? Who do you give a ride to in your car? Who do you set a place for at your dinner table? Could you promise yourself that you will no longer give that person the power to poison your precious personal time? When you leave school, that person stays there, and never again will you welcome them into your home or head.

Are you thinking, "I've tried to get this person out of my mind and I can't stop thinking about them"? Chances are you're telling yourself, "I'm *not* going to let that person make me mad" or "I've got to *stop* letting her get to me." Those admonitions contain the word "not" and "stop" which your mind doesn't hear, so you continue to think about the very person you don't want to think about.

Here are three ways we can take back control of our emotions instead of giving challenging individuals the power to ruin our peace of mind.

Peace of Mind Step #1: Ask Yourself, "Can I Change This?"

> "Give us the grace to accept with serenity the things that cannot be changed, courage to change the things which should be changed, and the wisdom to distinguish the one from the other."
> —Reinhold Niebuhr

Think of someone who's "driving you nuts." When we're unhappy with how someone is treating us, there are three things we can do about it.

- **Change the other person.** (Ha ha ha)
- **Change the situation.** Before we tell this person off or quit our job in frustration, we want to ask ourselves, "Is what's waiting for me a *trade up*?" If not, walking away is rash, not wise. In our foolhardy anger or haste to leave an unhappy situation, we may end up in another that's even worse.
- **Change yourself.** This is always an option, as it is completely within our control to accomplish. Leo Tolstoy said, "Everyone thinks of changing the world, no one thinks of changing himself." The good news is, in the process of changing ourselves (whether we become more assertive or focus on the positive aspects of the relationship) we often influence how the other person treats us.

Do you recall Martha, from the beginning of this chapter? Martha knew she wasn't going to be able to change the department head [said before woman was "department head," not dean]. The woman was known for her brusque manner. Other professors had approached her before in an attempt to forge a better relationship and had been brushed aside. Martha wasn't willing to change the situation. She loved teaching, loved this university, and wasn't willing to walk away from a secure job because of her sour relationship with her department head. Martha realized she was going to have to change herself.

One thing she did was reframe her feelings for her boss . I had told Martha, "In a long-term relationship, we tend to overvalue what someone is not, and undervalue what they are." Martha realized she had focused on all the things the department head was not. She was *not* friendly, democratic, or encouraging. On the other hand, she was organized, a decisive leader, and had lobbied rigorously for department funds.

Martha decided to appreciate her hard work on behalf of the department, put her brusque manner in perspective, and focus on her contributions instead of her criticisms.

Peace of Mind Step #2: Establish a Moan and Groan Moratorium

"Dost thou love life? Then do not squander time, for that is the stuff life is made of." —Benjamin Franklin

Martha continued, "Something else that helped was my husband and I agreed to a 'moan and groan moratorium.' My husband works a stressful job too, so we'd end up spending half the night swapping horror stories about the latest insult to injury. It was doing neither of us any good.

"My husband and I decided that when we got home, we'd each have fifteen minutes to vent. We could gripe about anything we wanted and get it off our chest. When our fifteen minutes was up, that was it. There are tons of more pleasant things for us to talk about. Our home is an oasis now instead of just another extension of the office.

"And the final thing I did to help me keep things in perspective was fill out my 'Calendar of Comments' on a daily basis."

Peace of Mind Step #3: Focus on What's Right vs. What's Wrong

"Instead of seeking new landscapes, develop new eyes."
—Marcel Proust

"What's this about a calendar?" you ask.

This is one of the most tangible ways we can move our focus off someone who's trying to take up residence in our brain. Buy a beautiful calendar and hang it in your office or classroom at school. Make sure the calendar features photos of something you like looking at—whether it's horses, tropical beaches, or Gary Larson's *Far Side* cartoons.

Resolve to write down one thing a day that goes right. This could be:

- A laugh you shared with a fellow teacher in the parking lot on the way in
- A student who was struggling with dyslexia had a breakthrough
- Your class surprised you with a cake on your birthday
- A student you coached won the city spelling bee competition
- A parent who volunteered to help out in class recognized and complimented your dedication and hard work
- A shy student found the courage to speak up in class for the first time
- Your new teacher's aide volunteered to come in on the weekend to help you decorate your classroom
- The principal supported your proposal to take a field trip

If you're a teacher, you may choose to rotate the responsibility for each day's comment amongst your class members. The daily entry doesn't have to be long—just long enough to trigger the memory. The only other rule is that it has to be legible so anyone wanting to read the calendar can do so.

Be sure to post this "Calendar of Comments" where you'll see it frequently throughout the day. Why does this have the power to help us keep our peace of mind?

Think of your mind as a camera and your eyes as the lens. Most of the time we are in wide-angle lens mode. We can think and do many things at once—and actually operate quite efficiently this way. A teacher can be writing on the chalk board while keeping an eye on Johnny in the back row, while thinking that recess is in ten minutes and there's a lot of material to cover, while reminding herself to pass out the permission slips before everyone leaves for the day.

When we're unhappy, though, we are unhealthily focused on one incident or individual. We're thinking, "I can't believe she said that to me," or "The nerve of that guy." As long as we continue to be outraged by a person's behavior, we continue to give them the power to upset us. The way to stop thinking about that person is to switch our attention to our calendar, which moves us back to wide-angle lens focus. We immediately become aware of all that's right with our world, instead of this one thing that's wrong. We turn griping into gratitude.

Post Your Calendar of Comments Where You'll See It

"What a wonderful life I've led. I only wish I'd realized it sooner."
—Colette

One teacher told me, "This calendar keeps me in the profession. I'm sure many teachers have told you they feel overworked, underpaid, and underappreciated. I have a master's degree in education, and I am entrusted with people's children (who should be our most precious possession and important priority), yet garbage collectors make more money than I do.

"We live in an area where the temperature gets to 90 to 100 degrees May through September. We don't have air-conditioning, so we have to keep our windows open. We're building a new wing onto the school, and the construction noise makes it almost impossible to concentrate. I go to my bank and get cash in air-conditioned comfort with luxurious carpets on the floor. I go to school and we have to wipe the grime off our desks every morning. We take better care of our money than we do our children.

"Half my students have asthma or respiratory problems because of the dust, and we can hardly hear each other. A number of my children are in Head Start, which means they at least get breakfast and lunch, however I don't know what or if they're eating when they leave here. English is the second language for almost a third of my students, and I frequently need to stop and repeat things so they can follow what I'm saying.

"I could go on," she said, "This is just the tip of the iceberg. So, why do I stay? I stay for the light bulb."

She saw my bewilderment and explained, "I stay for the light that goes on in the students' eyes when they 'get' it. I stay for the times they're struggling to make sense of something, but they stick with it and all of a sudden their faces light up, and I know they understand. I stay for the times they come up and give me a hug because they know it will be welcome. I stay for the times I run into one of them at the store and they run over and tell me how they're doing. I stay for the quiet ones who would get ignored if I didn't 'see' them and let them know how and why they're special.

"My calendar reminds me of all that. About the time I'm ready to quit because I'm fed up with some stupid paperwork that's got to be filled out in triplicate, I look at my calendar and things are okay again."

Abraham Lincoln said, "Most people are about as happy as they make up their minds to be." What are you going to do to keep a positive perspective? How are you going to keep control of your peace of mind instead of giving other people the power to poison it? Vow to try at least one of these ideas and you can make up your mind to be happy instead of harboring grudges and resentments that undermine the satisfaction of your valuable work.

Tongue Fu! Tip for Teens

One college student told me, "I wish every high school student could read this. One of the reasons I love college is, no *high school drama!*"

"What do you mean by that?" I asked.

"The nonstop gossip," she answered. "You couldn't go anywhere without hearing that so-and-so dropped so-and-so, and now she's dating his best friend, so he's spreading vicious rumors about her, so now none of her friends will talk to him, and on and on. We used to spend hours IM'ing each other every night or talking on our cells, getting worked up about the silliest things.

"We 'hated' our parents if they wouldn't let us stay out past curfew. A zit was the end of the world. If a girl dared to wear the same outfit twice in the same week, she got trashed. Everything was life and death. I can't believe how mean we were to each other."

"What do you wish you knew back then?" I asked her, "Or what do you wish you could tell teenagers now that you're 'older and wiser'?"

She replied, "I know some teenagers would think it's silly, but I think it would be great if they'd keep that calendar. Some kids keep a journal, but that takes so much time. It would only take a few seconds to write something on the calendar, and it would offset all the other petty junk we got so upset about.

"When I look back, I had a pretty good life; however, you'd never have known it at the time. I went to bed crying many nights because of something someone said to me. I obsessed about being 'chunky' (all of ten pounds overweight!), and that I wasn't part of the 'in' crowd. There was so much right with my life, but I failed to see it. My parents were actually pretty cool, I had good friends, and I was involved with the school newspaper. If I could go back, or give one piece of advice to other teens, it'd be to appreciate what you have, because there's probably a lot right with your life that you're not even seeing."

Put this book down for a minute. What are three specific things you like about your life? Who are three people you're grateful to have in your life? What are three aspects of your life you're glad for—but sometimes take for granted? Hopefully, just thinking about these got your mind off an aggravating person or situation, and reminded you that there's probably a lot more right with your life than wrong.

Action Plan for Maintain a Positive Perspective

As a principal, your day is one crisis after another. Some vocal parents are protesting your school's drug education program and are taking their case to the local newspaper and media. They're calling for your resignation and their constant criticism of your leadership is taking a toll. What do you do?

Words to Lose	Words to Use
You tell yourself that these people make you so mad. *"Don't these parents know the drug program is mandated?! They're blaming me and it's not my fault!"*	You remind yourself people can't make you mad unless you let them. *"They're entitled to their opinion. I'm going to set up a meeting so we can explain the program."*

Words to Lose	Words to Use
You allow yourself to focus on the individuals or incidents that are making you unhappy. *"They are attacking my character and harming my hard-earned reputation."*	You focus on all that's right with your job and everyone for whom you're grateful. *"I appreciate those principals calling me to show their support."*
You focus on everything that's going wrong. You start losing perspective and think about quitting. *"Why do I put myself through this? I could be making twice as much money with half the grief somewhere else."*	You start writing down on your calendar what's going well and it puts things in perspective. *"Just in the last week, we have lots to celebrate. This is Ann's twenty-first year here, and our new pool got approved."*
You take your frustration home with you and it becomes an extension of the office. *"It's 11 o'clock and I'm still wound tight."*	You establish a "moan and and groan moratorium" so you can enjoy your evenings. *"Okay, that's it. On to more pleasant subjects."*

29

"One's philosophy is not best expressed in words, it is expressed in the choices we make. In the long run, we shape our lives and we shape ourselves. The process never ends until we die. And the choices we make are ultimately our responsibility."

—Eleanor Roosevelt

Choose to Act and Influence with Integrity

A fundamental theme of Tongue Fu! is that, as Eleanor Roosevelt expressed above, we have a choice in how we communicate with others; we have a choice in how we treat others; and we have a choice in how we respond to others. And the choices we make have enormous power to shape our relationships and the quality of our lives—negatively or positively.

A teacher once told me, "I agree with everything you've talked about in this seminar. Sometimes though, it's hard to 'take the high road,' when other people aren't. Any suggestions on how we can stay committed to doing and being our best when circumstances are less than ideal?"

What's Your Why?

"He who has a why to live can bear almost any how."
—Friedrich Nietsche

Years ago, I was contracted to conduct training for a state agency. The director of this understaffed and overworked division said they were eighteen months behind in the recording and filing of some forms. Every weekday, dozens of people with documents lined up outside, hours before their doors even opened. I asked the director how she kept going in the face of such depressing conditions. She said, 'You've got to have a philosophy!' "

Wise woman. What's your philosophy—your "first thought" when something goes wrong? If it's, 'Not again, why do these things always happen to me?' it will set up a victim mentality where we persistently perceive we're the injured party. On the other hand, if it's "This too shall pass," we will be able to keep even the most distressing events in perspective.

Does your first thought serve you or sabotage you? The goal of this chapter is to share philosophies that can help us stay committed to handling challenging circumstances with integrity and equanimity, so that from now on when we're facing adversity, our philosophy kicks in for the better rather than for the worse.

Develop a Philosophy That Helps You through the Hard Times

"Our greatest freedom is the freedom to choose our attitude."
—Victor Frankl

You may already be familiar with Frankl's moving story. Frankl survived the Holocaust and wrote about his experiences in the book *Man's Search for Meaning*. This slim volume was selected by the American Library Association as one of the ten most significant books ever written. In it, Frankl concludes that we can't always choose or control what happens to us; we *can* choose how to respond to it.

Frankl certainly didn't choose to be held prisoner in a concentration camp, and he didn't choose to be treated so cruelly and inhumanely. When he was finally freed, he chose not to become a bitter man or harbor hatred. He chose to dedicate his life to making a positive difference for his fellow human beings.

I introduce Frankl's philosophy in every single Tongue Fu! program because I think it's the cornerstone of a mentally healthy lifestyle.

Though we can't always select what happens to us—crowded classrooms, lack of support, restrictive policies—we can select how to respond.

Little did I know that a frightening yet ultimately undeniable demonstration of this philosophy in action would come from our son Tom. To celebrate the last game of the Little League baseball season, we went to a local restaurant for dinner. We were enjoying the boys' debriefing of their up-to-bats when the waiter reached across our table to refill my coffee. His feet slipped out from underneath him and he spilled the pot of boiling black coffee all over us. I started screaming because I didn't know anything could be that hot. Tom was wailing in pain because the coffee had saturated his thick baseball pants and was scalding his body.

We quickly removed Tom's clothes, but not before the coffee had stripped the skin off his legs and caused second-degree burns. On the ambulance ride to the hospital, Tom kept crying, "Why me? I wasn't doing anything wrong. Why did this happen?" All we could do was comfort him while the emergency room doctors administered medication and dressed his wounds.

The day after his unfortunate incident, Tom's younger brother stayed home from school (big sacrifice) and spent hours solicitously bringing out games and patiently catering to Tom's every need. The following day, Tom's teacher stopped by to drop off a marvelous basket of letters and drawings from his classmates saying, "We miss you." "Hurry back." "It's no fun without you." It meant so much to Tom to receive this unexpected and welcome affirmation from his fellow students that he was well liked.

Fortunately, Tom recovered fully with no scars. He now looks back on that experience with the gut knowledge that *good things can and do come out of bad things*. He will carry that wisdom with him the rest of his years.

"Why Me?" Equals "Woe Is Me"

"Life is a game of cards. The hand that is dealt you represents determinism; they way you play it is free will." —J. Nehru

When things go wrong, our almost automatic reaction is "Why me?" If we continue to lament our fate with angry entreaties—"I don't deserve this," "This isn't fair"—we will continue to feel victimized and see the world as a harsh environment where innocent people are besieged by bad things.

We can play a hand more positively by asking, "Where's the good?" One of life's most important insights is to know with our heart and soul, as Tom does, that good things can come out of bad—and that good things can exist at the same time as bad. This is not to say that bad things are good. You may have been presented with bleak circumstances that were in no way positive; however, you can still reap positive things as a result of them. The good may not be apparent at the time. If you search for it or take responsibility for creating it, it can emerge.

In his thought-provoking book *No Ordinary Moments*, author and friend Dan Millman postulates that the issues we face are the spiritual weights we lift to strengthen ourselves. He believes our task is to shine through the petty annoyances of our life, to not become preoccupied with them. He says, "At the moment of your death, your whole life will pass before you. In a few fractions of a second—because time no longer applies—you will see many incidents from your life in order to learn. You will review your life with two questions in your consciousness: Could I have shown a little more courage in those moments? Could I have shown a little more love?"

Commit to a Higher Ideal

"There is only one thing that remains to us, that cannot be taken away: to act with courage and dignity and to stick to the ideals that give meaning to your life." —J. Nehru

Ideal is defined as "a standard of excellence; an ultimate object of aim of endeavor." Integrity is defined as "firm adherence to a code of moral values."

When conditions are discouraging, in moments of despair, we have to have some "ideal" or commitment to "integrity" to carry us through. Over the years, audiences have contributed dozens of different philosophies that have helped them handle challenges with courage, integrity, and love. A fellow trainer reacts to disappointment with a lilting "Oh well" and she's off to other activities.

For many people, the guideline that governs their actions is the Golden Rule, "Do unto others as you would have them do unto you." In her excellent book *Feel the Fear and Do It Anyway*, author Susan Jeffers recommends you repeat the words "I can handle it" whenever you encounter adversity. This phrase works as a mantra you can use to steady yourself in the face of threatening circumstances. Those four words can create a feeling of confidence ("I can") instead of cynicism ("I can't.")

Ann Landers advises readers to "expect trouble as an inevitable part of life and repeat to yourself the most comforting words of all, 'This, too, shall pass.' Despair is defined as the utter loss of hope." Instead of wallowing in despair when things go wrong, we can look at our Calendar of Comments and remember that our trials are temporary and we have plenty of things to be grateful for, and plenty of reasons to hope for better tomorrows.

One of the primary reasons we have hope for better tomorrows is that, as educators, we have unique opportunities to live a life that matters on a daily basis.

Remind Yourself That You're Making a Difference

"The purpose of life isn't to be happy; it's to matter, to feel it has made some difference that we have lived at all." —Leo Rosten

I was visiting my dad while on a speaking tour on the West Coast. He went out to get the mail and started sorting through it while we were sharing a cup of coffee. He opened one letter and read it silently. I noticed then that he was just sitting there quietly, tears in his eyes. "Uh-oh," I thought, "it's bad news." "What is it, Dad?" I asked.

He passed me the letter and motioned that it was okay to read it. It was from a former student. Dad was then Director of Vocational Agriculture Education for the state of California; however, for many years he had served as a shop and agriculture teacher for a small high school in Southern California.

The letter said, "You may not remember me, but I remember you. I was in your welding class fifteen years ago. I had been labeled as a troublemaker and everyone else had given up on me. I took your welding class just to bide time until I could legally drop out of school.

"That first week, you told us our semester project was going to be a four-animal stock trailer, and that we were going to make it together from scratch. I thought you were crazy. After teaching us the basics, you put us to work. Those fifty minutes in shop every day was the only time I ever enjoyed school. I'll never forget the first time we loaded some horses into the trailer to transfer them to another pasture and you asked me to drive. I remember looking in the rearview mirror and thinking, 'We built this. We built this.' It was the first time I was ever proud of anything I'd done in my life.

"You probably don't know this, but I make my living as a welder. The skills you taught me that semester have supported my wife, our two children, and me. Thanks to your belief in me, I hope to put my two kids through college with the income I earn from welding. Just thought you'd like to hear that one of your shop students made good. Thanks."

Doing Work That Matters Is the Most Important Motivator and Reward

> "What is the use of living if not to strive for noble causes and to make this muddled world a better place for those who will live in it after we are gone." —Winston Churchill

"The great use of life," said William James, "is to spend it for something that outlasts you." As educators, we have daily opportunities to change lives. That is not a grandiose statement, it is a fact.

Why should we continue to care when it sometimes seems other people don't? Why should we put in the long hours when it sometimes seems no one notices? Why should we continue to work in a profession that sometimes doesn't get the respect it deserves?

The answer to that is in the light in our students' eyes when they "get" something for the first time. The answer is in the knowledge they learn from us that helps them become contributing citizens. The answer is in the passion they developed for a topic because of our enthusiasm for it. The answer is in the decision-making ability they acquire because we hold them accountable for results. The answer is in the careers they pursue because we introduced them to a field of study that lit their mind on fire.

In the midst of the daily trials and tribulations, it's important to remind yourself that your work *does* matter. Yes, it is rewarding to get the letters; it is heartwarming to have the students come up to us years later and tell us how we made a difference for them; it is gratifying to see the progress from the beginning of the school year to the end of the school year.

However, we cannot rely on these external offerings of appreciation, or else our satisfaction and motivation will be dependent on favorable feedback. In the long run, it can't matter whether we receive the outward rewards, because those are fickle and often not proportionate to the effort invested. What we need to do is recommit ourselves on a daily basis to acting with integrity, caring for our students, getting along with our fellow educators, and knowing in our hearts that we're doing good work that matters.

John Gardner said, "Some people strengthen their society just by being the kind of people they are." Vow to strengthen yourself, your students, your peers, your school, and your society by being the *kind* of person who acts and influences with integrity.

Tongue Fu! Tip for Teens

Hopefully, you've learned a variety of ways to communicate more constructively so you can get along better with the people you encounter at school, at home, and in your community. Of everything you've learned, this following quote is one of the most important to understand and embrace.

Albert Schweitzer said, "I don't know what your destiny will be, but one thing I know: the only ones among you who will be really happy are those who have sought and found how to serve."

How do you serve others? How are you contributing? Would you like to know something you could do *today* to make this a better place for others?

Who is someone who has positively impacted you? Who is someone who has encouraged you, challenged you, and believed in you? An immediate way you can make a difference for others is to reach out to the people who've made a difference for you and thank them for what they did.

This could be a parent, teacher, minister, coach, counselor, relative, neighbor, librarian, principal, or peer. Take five minutes to write them a letter, give them a call, or speak to them face to face.

Be specific. What exactly did they say or do that impacted you? William James said, "The deepest desire in human nature is the craving to be appreciated." By letting this individual know exactly how he or she influenced you and by expressing your appreciation, you positively impact that person.

Don't assume they know how you feel. I went to a fiftieth wedding anniversary celebration where relatives and friends had gathered from around the country. The festivities included music, dancing, a video featuring highlights of the couple's life together, and many testimonials as people stood and told their favorite story about the couple. At the end of the tributes, the wife turned to her husband and said, "This has been the most wonderful day of my life. But I still haven't received the one thing I want most."

"What's that?" he asked. "You haven't told me you loved me," she said. Her husband of fifty years looked at her and kidded, "I married you, didn't I?" When his wife's face fell, he realized this was no joking matter. He caught himself, gave her a warm hug, and said, "I love you, Rose." After a half century of marriage, she still wanted to hear the words.

Think of what the people around you do on your behalf. Could one of them be waiting to hear the words? Are you thinking, "They know how I feel"? They don't, unless you tell them. George Eliot said, "I like not only to be loved, but to be told I am loved." The people who care about you and contribute to you are yearning to know that you recognize and appreciate all they do for you. Tell them or write them today. You will never regret doing it—you will only regret not doing it.

Action Plan for Choose to Act and Influence with Integrity

A parent has just threatened to sue you because of alleged "racial discrimination" against her son. This is a blow because you care for all your students, regardless of ethnicity. You feel this claim is groundless, yet you will have to spend time and money defending yourself. What do you do?

Words to Lose	Words to Use
You become demoralized and defeated and feel like giving up. *"I'm quitting. This puts me over the edge. It's so unfair."*	You have a philosophy that keeps you going in times of adversity. *"I will put this in perspective and focus on doing my best each day."*

Words to Lose	Words to Use
You wonder why you care so much when it doesn't seem appreciated. *"Why am I knocking myself out for this school when they're not backing me up?"*	You continue to care because you're committed to being a quality person. *"Wait a minute. I'm not letting this derail me from what I'm trying to achieve."*
You let your frustrating circumstances undermine your commitment to making a difference. *"I'm just going to put in my time and become a time clock puncher."*	You remind yourself that you're still making a difference despite these discouraging circumstances. *"I will focus on that great discussion we had yesterday in class."*
You bitterly question why you work so hard to act with integrity when it seems others aren't. *"No more weeknights and weekends for me. I'm doing the bare minimum from now on."*	You vow to act and influence with integrity because you want to lead a life that matters. *"I feel privileged to have a daily chance to change lives. That's what I'm going to stay focused on."*

PART V

Summary and Epilogue

"Let us, then, be up and doing . . ."

—HENRY WADSWORTH LONGFELLOW

30

"All the beautiful sentiments in the world weigh less than a single lovely action."

—James Russell Lowell

Turn Intentions into Actions

Have you ever finished a book all fired up, ready to go out and change the world, and two weeks later everything was back to "same old, same old"?

Please don't let that happen with this book. My business is called Action Seminars/Consulting because I believe the object of education isn't knowledge, it's action. Information doesn't have the power to change our life for the better until it's applied.

Identify Your Top Priority

"If you don't know where to begin, you don't begin."
—George S. Patton

A teacher told me, "I'm feeling overwhelmed. I'd like to apply all these suggestions at once, and I know that's not realistic. Any suggestions on how and where to get started?"

Good point. Confusion immobilizes. Clarity energizes. The purpose of this last chapter is to help you clarify your priorities and plan your follow-up so you produce real-world results. The best way to do that is to select *one* of the most relevant concepts for your circumstances. Then, write exactly how you plan to apply it, and post this reminder in a prominent place so you're frequently reminded of your commitment to put these principles into practice.

As Henry Ford, the father of the assembly line, observed, "Nothing is particularly difficult if you divide it up." You can become a Tongue Fu! black belt by incorporating these techniques into your daily life, one by one.

Please review this book. Skim through the pages and select a suggestion that is particularly timely for you. Write (if this is a library book, you can duplicate these pages and fill them out):

- **Why you like this idea:**
  I like the idea about listening rather than lecturing.
- **When you are going to put this idea into practice:**
  Starting Monday
- **How you are going to put this idea into practice:**
  I'm going to let students finish articulating their thoughts rather than impatiently cutting them off because I think I know what they want to say.
- **The hoped-for results of putting this idea into practice:**
  That way, I'll be more of a Socratic teacher who draws out students and helps them discover things on their own instead of trying to do it for them.

Tongue Fu! Idea #1

I like   _____

because   _____

Starting   _____

I'm going to   _____

That way,   _____

Not Sure You Can Change Years of Bad Habits?

"We can do anything we want, as long as we stick to it long
enough." —Helen Keller

A school maintenance supervisor raised his hand during the Q & A
period at the end of a program and said, "I'm fifty-five years old. I use
the words 'but,' 'problem,' and all the rest of them all the time. *I used
'em all in one sentence this morning.* These are so habitual for me, I
don't think I can change them. You know the old saying, 'You can't teach
an old dog new tricks.'"

"Glad you brought this up," I replied. "Can you remember the situation this morning where you used all the Words to Lose?"

"Sure," he said. "We had an electrical problem and I told my building engineer he needed to come in Saturday and Sunday to fix it. He
said, 'I can't come in this weekend, I've got family coming in from out of
town. I'm going to pick them up at the airport, and we've made plans.'

"I told him, 'I'm sorry you've got a *problem* with working this weekend, *but* you're going to have to because you're the only one who knows
the system. You *should* have told me earlier you couldn't come in.
There's nothing I can do about it now. *I can't* ask anyone else *because*
no one but you is qualified to do the job.' Man," he said remorsefully, "we
really got into it."

I said, "That's a perfect example of how there are many times we're
simply the messenger conveying the bad news. While we may not be
able to change the bad news, we *can* change the way we communicate
the bad news, which can change the way the other person responds to
the bad news and to us. Would you be willing to try a simple three
minute exercise that shows how we can teach (ahem) skeptical dogs
new tricks?" "Sure," he agreed.

Persevere through the Initial Awkward
Stage of Learning

"If at first you don't succeed, you're about average."
—slogan on coffee mug

See the line below? Please write on it, using your best handwriting, the sentence "I'm good at Tongue Fu!" (Once again, if this is a library or text book, please draw a line on a fresh piece of paper and write the sentence on that.)

Now, write the same sentence, ("I'm good at Tongue Fu!") on the line below—using your other hand.

How did it feel to write with that other hand? Awkward? Exactly. Would you agree that handwriting is a skill? Sure it is. None of us were born knowing how to write. We had to learn how to shape letters, form them into words, and construct sentences. How about playing tennis or using a computer? How about speaking a foreign language or playing an instrument? All of them are skills.

Did you know that when we learn any skill, or when we change any habit, we go through three stages? Interestingly, the three stages all begin with the letter A.

Awkward. When we try something new or different, it's uncomfortable, time consuming, and labor intensive. Do you remember the first time you drove a car with a stick shift? Do you remember stopping, starting, and stalling as you familiarized yourself with the clutch and gearshift? You didn't give up in frustration, though ("I'm a terrible driver. What made me think I could drive? I'll never do that again!"). You reassured yourself that your imperfect performance was to be expected. ("Of course I didn't drive very smoothly. I've never done it before. I'll get better if I just keep practicing.") You accepted that it would take awhile to work through the clumsiness and get good at it.

Applying. In this second stage, if you keep practicing and combining the techniques you've been taught, you get better results. You're coordinating the gas pedal, brake, and clutch while changing gears—without giving yourself whiplash. You're getting better at integrating the different elements and performing them smoothly and effectively. The skill still doesn't come fluidly or seamlessly yet, however your continued practice is paying off with improved performance.

Automatic. Voila! You have invested the time and effort to learn and practice the different elements of this skill, and it's paid off. You can now perform this new activity naturally and effectively. You're a skilled driver who gets from point A to point B without even having to think about clutches and gear shifts, because you've assimilated the steps until they're second nature. You've added this skill to your repertoire and are reaping the benefits of persevering through the three stages of the learning process.

Practicing These Tongue Fu! Techniques Will Pay Off

"Failure is the path of least persistence." —slogan on coffee mug

Are you wondering, "What's this got to do with Tongue Fu!?"

Wouldn't you agree that Tongue Fu! is a skill? As with any other skill, it takes time to master. It may initially feel awkward using *and* instead of *but*, and you're frustrated because you keep using it as a space filler when you pause to think. A teacher's aide may have let the students out early for recess, and before you can stop yourself, you tell her she *shouldn't* have done that—instead of clarifying that *from now on*, could she please be sure to wait for the bell before letting the kids go outside. A parent may complain that you didn't answer her e-mail, and you start explaining why you've gotten behind instead of taking the AAA Train.

That doesn't mean you'll never "get" this. That doesn't mean you might as well give up. That means you're in the to-be-expected first and second stages of changing old communication habits and adopting new ones. Please persevere through those initial awkward stages of applying these Tongue Fu! techniques. Be patient with yourself, keep your reminder cards where you'll continue to see them so you can "catch and correct," and continue to apply these suggestions at school, at home, and in your community.

You'll find that, over time, you no longer answer requests for assistance with "Sure, what's the problem?" which mistakenly gives the other person the impression that the only reason he or she should want to talk to you is because something is wrong. If faculty members are arguing about a new policy, you'll intervene with a "Let's not do this," and help the group focus on solutions rather than fault. If you're having "one of those kind of days," you'll look at your Calendar of Comments, remember your philosophy, and recommit to being the kind of person you want to be—no matter what.

Ready, Set, Grow!

"Happiness isn't a goal. It's a byproduct." —Eleanor Roosevelt

Getting along with people isn't a goal, it's a byproduct. It's a byproduct of communicating constructively so we can prevent conflicts and promote cooperation. It's a byproduct of choosing to respond instead of react so we can establish rapport instead of resentment. It's a byproduct of using these Tongue Fu! techniques so we can diplomatically disarm disputes and move toward agreement. It's a byproduct of, on a daily basis, acting and influencing with integrity so we can make a positive difference for others.

Adlai Stevenson advised, "Knowledge alone is not enough. It must be leavened with magnanimity before it becomes wisdom." John Ruskin noted something similar when he observed, "When love and skill go together, expect a masterpiece."

It is my fondest hope that you leaven your knowledge and application of these Tongue Fu! techniques with love and skill so you become a master of peace.

Tongue Fu! Tip for Teens

According to Thomas Edison, "Our greatest weakness lies in giving up. The most certain way to succeed is to always try just one more time." I hope you will at least try these ideas, because they're their own best reward. If you're like my sons, niece, and the other teenagers who've participated in Tongue Fu! programs across the country, you'll get such good responses, that you'll be motivated to continue to learn and apply these ideas.

I'll always remember the time my sons and I went to our local video store to get a video for a Friday night at home. We made our selection and stood in line to pay the cashier. She rang up our account and announced that we had $39 in late fees. Yikes. I was sure we had turned in our previous rentals on time, but the clerk wouldn't budge. I finally paid the penalty and we went out to our van; however, that had been the final straw of a l-o-n-g day, and I was venting my frustration. Andrew listened for awhile and then said, "Mom, look around. Think of all that's right with your world. We're all healthy; we live in Maui. When you put this in perspective, it's no big thing."

Busted! This is exactly what I'd told my sons when they were upset— and Andrew had turned the tables on me. How could I continue to gripe in the face of such unassailable logic? It broke the mood and we went on to have a fun evening.

So, pick one of these ideas that is particularly relevant for you and try it next time something goes wrong. I close with two of my favorite quotes. One is author Graham Greene's observation that, "In every childhood, there is a moment when a door opens and lets the future in." I hope this book has opened a door to a better future for you—a future where you can communicate better with the people you care about.

The second quote is from Aldous Huxley who said, "There's only one corner of the universe you can be certain of improving, and that's your own self." From this day forward, if you don't like your circumstances or how other people are treating you, remember that the best, more direct way to improve the situation is to change the way you communicate with those people.

Keep this book handy so you can refer to it again and again. And commit to applying these Tongue Fu! techniques so you'll be able to get along better with just about anyone, anytime, anywhere.

Postscript

Have you developed your own ways to deal with difficult individuals without becoming one yourself? Do you have a technique you've taught students that's helped them communicate more constructively? Is there a philosophy that helps you be the kind of person you want to be—no matter what? Do you have a success story showing how you've applied these ideas at your school?

It means a lot to receive your feedback and know this book has made a difference for you. You're probably busy, so please know I appreciate you taking the time to contribute your ideas and suggestions. If you'll include your e-mail address or contact information, I'll answer your correspondence.

You are invited to visit my website, www.SamHorn.com, to review articles, an updated public workshop schedule, and/or order books and tapes. Feel free to contact me at the address below for information about the Tongue Fu! monthly newsletter and to arrange a training program for your school or business.

Are you interested in becoming a certified Tongue Fu! trainer so you can teach these trademarked techniques? We conduct Tongue Fu! Training Institutes across the country on a regular basis. Visit www.SamHorn.com for information on how you can become licensed to share these ideas with others. I look forward to hearing from you, and to adding you to our Tongue Fu! team.

About the Author

Sam Horn, president of Action Seminars/Consulting, has been helping individuals and organizations communicate better since 1981. Her books *Tongue Fu!, ConZentrate, What's Holding You Back?*, and *Take the Bully by the Horns* have been featured in *Publishers Weekly, Library Journal, Chicago Tribune, Investors Business Daily*, and *Readers Digest*, and have been endorsed by such best-selling authors as Stephen Covey and John Gray.

She is a frequent media guest who has been interviewed on dozens of radio and TV shows including National Public Radio and To Tell the Truth, where she and her Tongue Fu! team stumped the panel. She speaks frequently for school districts, educational organizations, national conventions, and for such government agencies and corporate clients as NASA, Holland America Cruise Lines, the IRS, Department of Education, and Hewlett-Packard. Sam was the top-rated speaker at the 1996 and 1998 International Platform Association conventions and was selected as the Capital Outstanding Speaker of the Year for 2003–2004. Executive Book Summaries said she has "added to the legacy of ideas on how to deal with people left by Benjamin Franklin, Abraham Lincoln, and Dale Carnegie."

One of her most satisfying accomplishments is sharing these ideas with educators so they can teach the next generation to communicate more constructively with others. People from around the world have attended the Tongue Fu! Training Institute to become certified in teaching Sam's trademarked methodology to their students, colleagues, employees, and audiences.

Want more information about Sam Horn's programs or products? Visit www.SamHorn.com, email info@SamHorn.com, or call 805-528-4351 to make arrangements for Sam to share these techniques with your group or to find out how you can become certified in Tongue Fu!

Do you have feedback about how these *Tongue Fu! at School* ideas have produced results in your relationships? Do you have questions about the application of these principles? Do you have your own suggestions on how we can get along better with anyone, anytime, anywhere? Sam would love to hear from you. Please contact us at www.SamHorn.com with your requests and recommendations.